# Botched Business

# Botched Business

The damaging process
of reorganising
local government
2006-2008

Michael Chisholm and Steve Leach

Douglas
McLean

Copyright © 2008 Michael Chisholm and Steve Leach

The authors' moral rights have been asserted


First published 2008 by

Douglas McLean Publishing
8 St John Street
Coleford
Gloucestershire
GL16 8AR


British Library Cataloguing in Publication Data
A catalogue record for this book is available from the British Library

ISBN 978-0-946252-69-5

Typeset in Garamond

10 9 8 7 6 5 4 3 2 1


Designed by Douglas McLean

Printed in Great Britain
by
Cromwell Press
Trowbridge
Wilts.

# Preface

We have not written this book to discuss the merits or otherwise of different structures of local government. What we have done is to give an account of our grave concern about the way central government proceeded in order to create a few more unitary councils in England. The Government acted as though the relevant legislation, the Local Government Act 1992, had been repealed when it had not, this being a matter on which the Court of Appeal expressed its reservations when hearing a judicial review. In addition, the manner in which the Government carried out the re-organisation process amounted to political deception and created a cascade of dishonesties, the impact of which will be felt for a long time after the immediate circumstances have faded into history. At the root of our concern is the following proposition. However good an objective may be, the achievement of that goal will be compromised in some degree if the means used to achieve the desired end are themselves wrong.

Local government is an essential part of the way in which the country is governed. To an approximation, local authority net current expenditure in England is £100 billion p.a., a figure equivalent to about 9% of England's Gross Domestic Product and roughly 20% of the United Kingdom's public sector current spending. With this money, local authorities provide a wide range of essential services, ranging from child protection to the collection and disposal of household refuse. They also have essential roles in handling planning applications, protecting the environment and maintaining public health standards. Equally important, although parish and town councils have a significant role locally, local authorities are the only substantial elected bodies below Parliament, able to represent the wishes of their citizens and to shape the circumstances of their lives. Therefore, they play an immensely important part in the maintenance of the proper checks and balances that are required in a democracy. Despite these important roles in the body politic, local authorities in Britain, and specifically in England, exist only by virtue of statute, with no protection constitutionally enshrined, as in many other countries.

There are two reasons for writing this book. First, what happens to local government is important in its own right, affecting as it may all citizens. Second, the way that the 2006-2008 local government re-organisation (LGR) in England was carried out should be troubling for everyone, as an example of the way that the Government chooses to treat its citizens and to obtain its way by means that can only be described as political deception. The Government rhetoric trumpets the virtues of transparency, accountability and involvement, but its actions in this case have belied the good words.

These may seem to be strong accusations to level against the Government. The pages that follow amplify the reasons for our concern, and the evidence upon which the concern is based. We have not attempted to provide a complete account of everything that occurred over a period of about 18 months, but we deal with the main issues and back that discussion with detailed evidence that is fully documented.

We both became involved in the 2006-2007 LGR independently the one of the other but our paths crossed in Cheshire. Leach had been asked to assist Crewe & Nantwich and Congleton, two Cheshire districts, to evaluate proposals for two different unitary options in that county with which they did not agree, and invited Chisholm to assist by examining the financial cases put forward by the proponents of the two schemes to replace the county and district system of two tier working. Leach was also working with the local authorities in Lincolnshire, preparing a bid for Pathfinder changes to two tier working in that county, which would see the continuation of the district and county councils. Meantime, Chisholm was requested by Devon CC to examine the unitary bid by Exeter, and by districts to do likewise in respect of the unitary submissions of their respective counties: Cornwall, Co. Durham, North Yorkshire, Shropshire, Somerset and Wiltshire.

Towards the end of 2007, we concluded that our concern about the way in which the Government had conducted the process was such that we could not walk away and say nothing. The account that follows shows that the 2006-2007 LGR holds a mirror to the way in which public life at all levels is conducted, and the image is not pretty.

We owe a very large debt of gratitude to those with whom we have worked during the LGR and who have assisted with writing this book. It would be impossible to name everyone who has contributed in one way or another, and for some individuals it would be potentially embarrassing to be named. We hope that no offence will be taken by those not included in the following short list: Ann Hamblin, Robin Hooper, David

Marren, Phil Morton, Andrew Pate, Robert Pettigrew, Vivienne Quayle, Kerry Rickards, Bob Smyth and Colin Wilby. Steve Leach wishes to acknowledge the cheerful and efficient support of Aileen Kowal in typing and amending his numerous handwritten contributions to the book. We are both very grateful to our publisher, Doug McLean, for the speed and efficiency of the publication process. Last but not least, our respective wives, Judith and Karen, have been unstinting in their understanding and forbearance.

*April 2008*

# Contents

# 1

# Introduction

We are deeply concerned about the process that was employed by the Department for Communities and Local Government (DCLG) and the impact of the outcome. This concern has been set out briefly in a recent paper examining the 16 decision letters on the unitary proposals that went forward for consultation. This paper led to the following conclusion: 'The process is so flawed that it corrupts the body politic' (Chisholm and Leach 2007, p. 17). Our present purpose is to set out more fully than was possible in the 2007 paper the reasons leading to our pessimistic conclusion.

The main feature of the reorganisation process that was initiated in October 2006 will be referred to by the abbreviation LGR, standing for local government reorganisation. Two tier local government was abolished in seven counties, with the creation of nine new unitary councils, and the prospect that there may be some more to come in the next few years. There was a parallel process, known as Pathfinder, for improving the operation of two tier local government; we will not discuss this, except incidentally. Barely a decade previously, there had been a review of all shire England, leading to the creation of 46 unitary councils, combining county and district functions, and the complete unitary reorganisation of local government in both Scotland and Wales. That bout of structural change had itself been preceded by major reorganisation in the 1970s and some substantial changes thereafter. What was extraordinary about the 2006-2008 LGR was the way it was conducted as if there were no history to which to refer. In our perception, this was a fundamental weakness of the whole process, casting a considerable blight upon the way in which matters were handled.

More immediately, the LGR was divorced from other aspects of contemporary government policy, or provides an apt commentary thereon. The Government makes much play with the need for financial probity in public spending, and the need to obtain 'value for money', but fails to live up to its own rhetoric, as shown by two recent parliamentary reports. Ministers have argued that recent large scale immigration has been economically beneficial for Britain, citing Treasury estimates that Gross Domestic Product (GDP) has been increased by £6 billion p.a. However, as the House of Lords Select Committee on Economic Affairs (2008) has pointed out, the relevant yardstick is GDP per person, preferably for the pre-existing population. On the evidence available, the Committee concluded that the effect of immigration on GDP per person has been close to zero. If that conclusion is correct, the economic benefit of immigration has been much less than the Government would have one believe.

More directly relevant to our own enquiry is another recent document. Following the 2004 report by Sir Peter Gershon, central government departments were set a collective target to achieve efficiency savings of £21.5 billion p.a. by 2007/08. As of September 2006, the Government claimed to have achieved savings of £13.3 billion p.a., but the Committee of Public Accounts (2007), House of Commons, judged that only one quarter of this sum was reliably accounted for. The reasons given for doubts about the remaining three quarters are instructive.

Altogether, the Committee identified eight reasons for querying the Government's claims about Gershon savings, of which two are particularly relevant for our study:

- Presentation of savings gross, ignoring off-setting costs.

- Use of inconsistent definitions.

Two other problems identified by the Committee may be mentioned, although little direct attention will be paid to them in the pages that follow:

- Inaccuracies in the baseline figures.

- Variations in the baseline dates chosen.

Four further problems are worth mentioning for completeness, but are not matters that concern us in the present context:

- Unintended decline in service quality.

- Inclusion of one-off savings.

- Use of estimates or projections instead of data on actual performance.

- Improvements had to be sustainable for only two years.

To give some idea of the serious nature of the concerns raised, two examples from the report are worth mentioning. First, the Department for Work and Pensions reported efficiency gains of £300 million p.a. but ignored off-setting costs of £164 million. Second, the Home Office claimed that it had achieved more than 90% of its efficiency target, at a time when the Home Secretary declared the Department 'not fit for purpose" (CPA 2007, pp. 10 and 13).

The Treasury has stated that, in future, it will report efficiency gains net of implementation costs. Although this commitment is to be welcomed, the evidence from the Committee of Public Accounts is that quite elementary concepts are overlooked or ignored by the Government as a routine matter of course. In other words, there has been, and continues to be, manifest incompetence in the management of public finances.

Another matter to consider is the speech given by the Prime Minister at the University of Westminster (*Telegraph* 26 October 2007), at the launch of a number of consultation documents. As reported, Mr Brown wished to throw off the authoritarian image that the Labour Government had acquired and to launch a new chapter in civil liberty, offering the possibility of a Bill of Rights and Duties and even a written constitution. In part, he was seeking to build upon ministerial pronouncements that there needs to be devolution of power from central government and that communities need to be empowered, the latter aspiration having been proclaimed in the October 2006 White Paper, *Strong and Prosperous Communities* (DCLG 2006a) that initiated the LGR.

Unfortunately, the DCLG has proved willing to accept unreliable financial estimates for the costs and savings to be expected from structural reorganisation, has been selective in the evidence to which it has given credence, and has failed to insist on proper devolved (or area) governance within large unitary authorities – whole counties in particular.

Although five criteria were set out in October 2006, it will become apparent that the Department, and hence the Secretary of State, deviated substantially from the rules initially established. Indeed, the Government got itself into something of a legal tangle over the whole process, a tangle that raised fundamental issues about the extent of, or limitations upon, the power of the nation's Executive. As a result, for most of the time the LGR proceeded, there was a parallel process in the courts leading to a hearing before appeal court judges, the outcome of which only became known in March 2008. There was a second and more restricted court case that we will also consider.

Although the 2006 White Paper had much to say about the empowerment of communities and neighbourhoods, the DCLG showed scant regard for the attitudes the public, and a curiously selective approach to the 'consultation' with those described as 'partners and stakeholders'. If politicians were to be serious about the perceived apathy of the electorate, they would take pains to ensure that consultation was genuine and not a charade.

The fundamental problem is that rhetoric has not matched practice, a fact that raises some basic issues not just for local government but also for the governance of the country in general. We believe that the issues raised by the LGR concern the nation as a whole, for what it reveals about the way in which the country is governed – or misgoverned. Consequently, we believe that the tale needs to be told, and told with sufficient detail to substantiate the dismal conclusion to which we have been forced by the evidence that we have encountered.

Our starting point is the view that an exercise as important as the LGR ought to have been conducted by reference to four general criteria, which may be set out as the touchstones for what follows:

- The objectives are clear, and consistent with other relevant central government objectives.

- The rules of the game are clarified at the outset and are applied consistently throughout the process.

- Proposals are developed on the basis of a thorough review of the available evidence and using an appropriate methodology.

- The justification for the set of proposals is clear and consistent.

However, the procedures adopted by the DCLG fell a long way short of the standards enshrined in these criteria.

Something must be said about the structure of the book. By convention, there should be an introductory chapter recounting the recent history of local government re-organisation in England, covering at least the period since the Second World War. Such a chapter would place the 2006-2008 LGR in context. We have chosen to approach matters differently. A curious feature of the LGR is that it seems to have been undertaken with scant regard for history, other than the desire to avoid a damagingly long period of uncertainty. With this in mind, we plunge into the story, thereby, we hope, conveying some sense of what it felt like for those who were involved. Once the story has been told and the outcome explained, we briefly discuss the historical background as part of the attempt to understand what has been going on, and to provide insight for the future.

Therefore, Chapter 2 provides a factual account of the LGR, as the framework for the succeeding detailed discussion. The decisions to which the Government came, and the reasons given for those decisions, are discussed in Chapter 3, revealing inconsistencies and contradictions in the way the Government's own five criteria were applied. Three of those criteria can be examined against some reasonably 'hard' evidence, as in Chapters 4 and 5. The first of these deals with the financial cases for change, and therefore with the criteria of Affordability and Value for money; the second discusses the level of Support commanded by proposals. These two chapters reveal the inconsistent and selective approach of the DCLG.

The other two criteria adopted by the DCLG, Strategic leadership and Neighbourhood empowerment, are imprecise, little more than promissory statements of intent. Because they are difficult to pin down, 'evidence' about them is lacking and it is difficult to test the judgements of the Secretary of State as rigorously as is possible with the first three criteria. For this reason, although Strategic leadership and Neighbourhood empowerment played a significant part on the decision process, we have not accorded them a separate chapter. Discussion about these two issues is contained in the other chapters, particularly Chapters 3 and 4.

Judicial review proceedings brought by Shrewsbury and Congleton are discussed in Chapter 6. In the event, their application was rejected by the Court of Appeal, but the case raised some important general issues that are highly relevant for the governance of the country. Chapter 7 deals briefly with another judicial review, initiated by Bedfordshire CC, which was also lost but raised important matters. Chapter 8 examines the LGR decisions, how they may be explained and their significance for the future of local government, including a brief historical account. The final chapter concentrates on the generally damaging effects of the way in which the Government proceeded with the LGR, the liberties it has taken and the political deception employed.

At the time of completing this book, there was still some unfinished business. Three cities – Exeter, Ipswich and Norwich – submitted proposals to become unitary authorities in counties that would otherwise retain the county and district structures. These proposals have been referred to the Boundary Committee for their advice, with the instruction to the Committee to consider the whole of the respective counties for possible unitary structures. The outcome of these considerations will not be known for some time to come. However, we see little advantage in waiting, because the reasons for writing this book will not be affected in any way by the outcomes, nor will the evidence we have used change. The relevant chapter of history closed with the Bedfordshire judicial review judgment, which became available on 4 April 2008.


**Authors' note:**
Where we quote from identified sources and wish to emphasise certain words or phrases, we have done so by underlining. There was no such emphasis in the originals.

# 2

# The reorganisation process
# from October 2006 onwards

The unitary ball was set rolling with the publication in October 2006 of the White Paper *Strong and Prosperous Communities* (DCLG 2006a). As part of the modernisation agenda, councils would be invited to submit bids to become unitary councils, or, alternatively, to improve two tier working, and the invitation was issued at the same time as the White Paper (DCLG 2006b). Bids for unitary status and for Pathfinder two-tier working were to be submitted by 25 January 2007, barely three months later. Ministers sought to emphasise the voluntary nature of the process:

> *It is wholly at the discretion of a council whether or not it responds to this invitation. The Government accepts that it is only in some areas that local government restructuring is widely seen as the way forward. It will be from councils in such areas that proposals are made. (DCLG 2006b, para. 2.8)*

With these words, the Department for Communities and Local Government asserted that structural change was not mandatory and proposals would come only from areas where there was general agreement that moving to unitary structures would be desirable. On the other hand, the Local Government and Public Involvement in Health Bill, published in December 2006, contained a provision for the Secretary of State to direct councils to prepare proposals, a power which lapsed on 25 January 2008 under the Act as finally passed. There was in fact no direction issued, but the implicit threat went some way to undermine the DCLG's assertion that the preparation of proposals was 'wholly at the discretion' of councils. The DCLG itself would handle the whole process – from the issuing of the invitation, receipt of proposals, decisions on which proposals would go forward for consultation and final decisions regarding restructuring. Table 2.1 shows that July 2007 had been pencilled in for the announcement of final decisions, an intention reinforced by the following passage:

> *The Government intends to announce, by the end of July 2007, which proposals will proceed to implementation* (DCLG 2006b, para. 5.14).

This intention was reiterated in April 2007, in a document entitled 'Frequently Asked Questions', issued after the decision had been announced in March that 16 proposals were going forward for consultation.

Implementation of final decisions would depend upon new legislation. The clear intent was that decisions taken in July 2007 would be implemented, assuming that the requisite statutory power had been obtained, there being no implementation power under the then existing 1992 Act.

---

**Table 2.1**
Indicative decision timetable for creating unitary authorities,
set out in October 2006

| | |
|---|---|
| January 2007 | Deadline for councils to submit proposals for unitary structures. |
| March 2007 | Announcement of the Government's preliminary views as to those proposals that have met specified criteria. Consultation with local stakeholders that are potentially affected by proposals. |
| June 2007 | Stakeholder consultation closes. |
| Early July 2007 | Final announcement of those areas that will be restructuring into unitaries. |
| May 2008 | Elections to new unitaries. |
| By April 2009 | New unitaries up and running. |

Source: DCLG 2006b, para. 5.22.

## The Local Government Act 1992 as amended

Under the 1992 Act, the Secretary of State had the power to direct the Boundary Committee of the Electoral Commission to undertake a review of a specified two-tier area in England for the purpose of recommending whether there should be change to a unitary structure for part or all of the area and, if change were recommended, what the unitary structure should be. The Secretary of State could accept the recommendation (with or without modification) but could not substitute a different unitary structure. The Committee was responsible for seeking proposals and comments thereon, formulating draft proposals and consulting before coming to a conclusion. In so doing, the Committee had to have regard to any advice or guidance that might be issued by the Secretary of State, and might employ consultants as appropriate. According to the Act, the Committee <u>must</u> provide information to, and consult with, 'persons <u>who</u> <u>may</u> be interested in proposals for an area'. This obligation was stated three times.

Manifestly, the procedure adopted by the Government in 2006 was radically different from that specified in the 1992 Act, with the implication that the Secretary of State did not possess the power to reach decisions and for these to be implemented, hence the need for new primary legislation. This procedural difficulty laid the ground for challenges to the process used by the DCLG, challenges that took the form of judicial review proceedings which ran in parallel with the restructuring process (see Chapters 6 and 7).

## The Local Government and Public Involvement in Health Act 2007

The Local Government and Public Involvement in Health Bill was published on 12 December 2006, completed its passage to the statute book late the following October and the provisions relevant for our purpose came into effect on 1 November 2007. Consequently, for much of the LGR process, the DCLG was acting on the assumption that the necessary powers would be forthcoming for implementation, and, indeed, that retrospective authority would be given for actions taken.

Acts of Parliament can differ materially from the terms of Bills as originally presented. In the present case, no significant changes were introduced for those parts of the legislation relevant for our purpose and it is therefore appropriate to explain the provisions set out in the Act rather than in the Bill.

The Act gave retrospective legitimacy for actions taken before 1 November 2007:

*It is immaterial that the invitation or guidance was given, the proposal made, or the consultation carried out, before rather than after the commencement of this Chapter* (2007 Act, Section 21(2)).

Note that this retrospective authority did not apply to the taking of decisions about whether or not to create a unitary authority. And note also that, in October 2006, it was the intention of the DCLG that final decisions would be announced in July of that year. The manner in which the Department tried to handle this procedural problem forms an important part of the story that unfolds.

Ministers have been at pains to insist that the 2006-2008 LGR was a 'window of opportunity' for unitary re-structuring, and a superficial reading of the 2007 Act would apparently confirm that claim. However, this 'window' was a time limited opportunity for the Secretary of State to direct local authorities to prepare unitary plans; the power to issue a direction lapsed on 25 January 2008. Looking ahead to the discussion in Chapter 8, the 2007 Act enables the Secretary of State to invite proposals and to implement them by Order, without recourse to the Boundary Committee (Section 7(1)(a)), with the implication that another 'window of opportunity' could be opened at any time.

Noteworthy at this juncture is the absence on any obligation on the Secretary of State to consult 'persons who may have an interest'. Instead, he must consult affected local authorities and 'such other persons as he considers appropriate'. The full implications of this change will become apparent as the account proceeds.

Finally, the whole concept of the LGR was that of competitive bidding. From the outset, it was said that no more than about eight unitary proposals would be accepted. Therefore, if the DCLG were to judge that the number of eligible proposals exceeded that limit, arrangements would have to be made to 'prioritise' proposals, i.e., put them into a rank order of priority. This approach meant that those preparing proposals had a strong incentive to present their cases as attractively as possible; the temptation to exaggerate the benefits and minimise the disadvantages of structural change was greater than it would have been in a non-competitive situation. That might not matter if the DCLG's scrutiny was sufficiently thorough.

By treating the LGR as a beauty competition the Government created the following problem. One or more councils could make a unitary proposal but, if the proposal succeeded, implementation would be for the successor authority, and there could be no certainty that the specific arrangements described in the bid documents would be put in place. The Government would have no direct power to force the new council to follow the bid proposal, which might in any case have been overtaken by other changes, either specific to the area or applying to local authorities in general. This was a weakness of the LGR that reinforced the temptation to exaggerate the benefits of change and minimise the disadvantages.

## The original five criteria for unitary reorganisation, October 2006

So that the matter can be followed step by step, it is appropriate to reproduce the five criteria set out in the October 2006 invitation to councils to submit unitary bids (DCLG 2006b, para. 3.1):

> *The criteria with which any proposal <u>must conform</u> are:*
>
> i)    *the change to the future unitary local government structures <u>must be</u>:*
>
> - *affordable, i.e. that change itself both represents value for money and can be met from councils' existing resource envelope; and*
> - *supported by a broad cross section of partners and stakeholders; and*
>
> ii)    *those future unitary local government structures must:*
>
> - *provide strong, effective and accountable strategic leadership;*
> - *deliver genuine opportunities for neighbourhood flexibility and empowerment; and*
> - *deliver value for money and equity on public services.*

However, the force of these criteria was reduced by a short passage that preceded the text reproduced above:

> *In submitting a proposal councils must <u>have regard</u> to the <u>guidance</u> set out in sections 3-6. Any proposal <u>should</u> conform to the criteria set out in section 3 of the guidance* (para. 2.6).

Henceforth, these criteria will be identified in abbreviated form, with a capital letter, for example, Value for money. As set out above, the clear intention was that any proposal must meet all five criteria. This was manifestly impossible for the first stage of the process, the submission of the original bids, which had to be lodged with the DCLG by 25 January 2007. Although drafts of some bids were in circulation before the deadline, the opportunity for comment thereon was extremely limited. It was impossible for any proper assessment of Support to be made in January 2007. The most that could be expected would be clarification of the level of Support by the time the consultation period (March to June) had ended.

Some further features of the criteria must be noted, particularly in the light of the amplification set out in paragraphs 3.2-3.11 in the DCLG invitation document. The first and the last of the criteria included the phrase 'value for money', so that the financial assessment appeared twice. This slovenly drafting gave rise to some oddities in the evaluation process. Problems were compounded by amalgamating two distinct concepts in the fifth criterion, 'value for money and equity on public services', concepts that cannot be directly combined in a meaningful way, and matters were made worse by including the requirement for communities to play 'an active role in influencing and shaping both planning and delivery of services.' As for the level of Support by partners and stakeholders, this was amplified to read 'key partners, stakeholders and service users/citizens', with the further statement that: 'The Government will consult on proposals that it is minded to implement prior to taking any final decisions'. Of Neighbourhood empowerment, it was said that 'there needs to be devolution of power down to local communities', with 'a strong citizen focus'.

According to the summary criteria reproduced above, a proposal must be 'supported by a broad cross section of partners and stakeholders', but members of the public were not mentioned. It was only in the amplification that public opinion and the attitudes of service users were mentioned, with the clear implication that their assessments would be less important than those of 'partners and stakeholders'. On the other hand, the fourth criterion emphasised 'neighbourhood flexibility and empowerment', a phrase that was then expanded to include improvement of 'the quality of life for citizens', 'citizen focus' and several other similar terms. With this emphasis upon citizen focus and participation, one could be forgiven for thinking that evidence about public attitudes to unitary proposals would have been important to the Government – how far was the public persuaded that these desirable goals would be realised? From the way that matters were set out in October 2006, it is clear that the DCLG was ambivalent about the role of public opinion in deciding whether or not restructuring should go ahead, and that ministers and officials were inclined to regard the public's views as unimportant.

The five criteria set out above were overlapping and muddled. With the elaborations expanding on the initial formulation, they became even more inadequate than was initially apparent. This poor drafting may have been unintentional, or it may have been deliberate: neither possibility encourages confidence in the DCLG. The poor drafting provided a dubious basis for the LGR exercise.

### The consultation and decision process

The DCLG allowed itself a bare two months in which to evaluate the twenty-six bids that were submitted towards the end of January 2007 before announcing which would go forward for consultation. During this time, letters were sent to all of the authorities that had put proposals forward, seeking clarification and/or explanation of matters in the documentation or that had not been included; Table 4.2 reproduces an

---

**Table 2.2**

Unitary proposals not proceeding to stakeholder consultation in March 2007

| | |
|---|---|
| Bedfordshire | Mid and South Bedfordshire unitary, proposed by two districts. |
| Cheshire | Three unitaries, proposed by two districts. |
| Cornwall | Single unitary, proposed by six districts. |
| Co. Durham | Pathfinder to unitary, proposed by five districts. |
| East Riding/ N. Yorks | Union of Selby with East Riding, proposed by East Riding. |
| Lancashire | Burnley and Pendle, proposed by Burnley and Pendle. Lancaster, proposed by Lancaster. Preston, proposed by Preston. |
| Oxfordshire | Three unitaries, proposed by Oxford. |
| Somerset | East Somerset, proposed by South Somerset. |

Sources: Letters dated 27 March 2007 to the relevant councils: *Hansard*, 5 December 2007, col. 67WS.

example, being the questions posed to Exeter; the three financial questions will be examined in some detail in Chapter 4. At this stage of the discussion, the point to note about the request to Exeter is the anodyne nature of the questions that were asked, a feature replicated in varying degree in the other letters. That the initial scrutiny was not rigorous will become especially clear in Chapter 4.

On the basis of this preliminary sifting, ten proposals were rejected as being too weak to warrant further consideration (Table 2.2) and the remaining sixteen went forward for consultation (Table 2.3). The relevant letters were sent out on 27 March, allowing three months for consultation on those that had cleared this first hurdle. All consultation material had to be submitted to the DCLG, and this body evaluated all the material before announcing decisions, which were made public on 25 July – as shown in Table 2.3.

Members of Parliament were told in July that the Secretary of State was 'minded to' implement nine proposals, if or when the Local Government and Public Involvement in Health Bill were enacted. The Written Statement from Mr John Healey said of these nine proposals that the Government could afford to implement them all, obviating the need to undertake a prioritisation exercise, and that:

> *These new unitaries, as they move towards implementation, will need to take into account our developing agenda for empowering citizens and communities and for stronger economic leadership …*

And

> *Implementing Bedford borough's proposal means that we must consider the future local government structures for the remaining county area. We are satisfied that this area needs unitary local government …*

It was also stated that:

> *Once implemented these nine proposals, on the basis of councils' current estimates, will save over £150 million annually. (Hansard 25 July 2007, col. 69WS.)*

It was indicated that further work was being requested on the financial cases for two unitary councils in Cheshire, and for the unitary Bedford, Exeter and Ipswich proposals. Despite this caveat, the whole tenor of the statement to Parliament was that decisions had been taken and that it was merely a matter of time before they would be implemented. The formula of being 'minded to implement' the proposals appeared to be meaningless, a matter of appearance, in that the decisions had been taken and all that was necessary was for the Bill to be enacted.

The DCLG issued a press release on 25 July, the phrasing of which was much more dogmatic than that used in Parliament:

> *Local Government Minister, John Healey, has today announced that nine proposals for unitary status will now go ahead towards implementation with the intention that all new authorities are fully up and running in 2009. …The proposals open the door to creating flagship councils that will lead the way on promoting prosperity, empowering citizens and communities, and improving public services for the 3.5 million people in the areas going forward. The number of councils in these areas will be reduced from forty-six to eleven.*

It was also said in the press release that certain proposals, including proposals for a single unitary council for the counties of Bedfordshire and Cheshire, 'will not proceed'.

The letters sent to the relevant authorities were more circumspect, seeking to avoid the impression that final decisions had been taken and emphasising their 'minded to' nature, as is illustrated by a passage in the letter to Wiltshire CC:

> *I am now writing to inform you that, in the Secretary of State's judgement, there is a reasonable likelihood that, if implemented, the proposal would meet the outcomes specified by each of the criteria set out in the invitation. Consequently, she is minded to implement your proposal if and when the Local Government and Public Involvement in Health Bill is enacted.*

Identical or similar wording was used in the other letters indicating the intention to proceed, and equivalent negative phrasing where the intention was not to implement the proposal, or, in the case of Norwich, to refer it to the Boundary Committee. Using the 'minded to' formulation, the Secretary of State sought to stick with the original timetable but to avoid taking final decisions for which she had no statutory power at that time.

With the 2007 Act on the statute book, Mr John Healey, the Minister for Local Government, in a written statement to Parliament on 5 December 2007, announced decisions for most of the proposals. There

## Table 2.3
### The DCLG's decisions, July 2007

The assessments of the five criteria are in the form of yes/no answers to the following question: Is there 'a reasonable likelihood that, if implemented, the proposal would meet the outcomes specified by each of the criteria set out in the Invitation?'

| The five criteria | A | B | C | D | E |
|---|---|---|---|---|---|
| *DCLG minded to implement* | | | | | |
| *No request for further work on finances* | | | | | |
| Cornwall unitary authority | Yes | Yes | Yes | Yes | Yes[1] |
| Co. Durham unitary authority | Yes | Yes | Yes | Yes | Yes[1] |
| Northumberland unitary authority | Yes | Yes | Yes | Yes | Yes[1] |
| Shropshire unitary authority | Yes | Yes | Yes | Yes | Yes[1] |
| Wiltshire unitary authority | Yes | Yes | Yes | Yes | Yes |
| | | | | | |
| *Request for further work on finances* | | | | | |
| Bedford unitary authority | Yes | Yes | Yes[1] | ?[2] | Yes[1] |
| Cheshire, 2 unitary authorities | Yes[1] | Yes[1] | Yes | ?[2] | Yes[1] |
| Exeter unitary authority | Yes[1] | Yes | Yes[1] | ?[2] | Yes |
| Ipswich unitary authority | Yes[1] | Yes | Yes | ?[2] | Yes |
| | | | | | |
| *DCLG minded not to implement* | | | | | |
| Bedfordshire unitary authority | Yes | Yes[1] | Yes | Yes | Yes |
| Cheshire unitary authority | Yes[1] | Yes | Yes | Yes | Yes[1] |
| Cumbria unitary authority | No[1] | No[1] | Yes | Yes | Yes[1] |
| Norwich unitary authority[3] | Yes | Yes | No | No | Yes |
| Northumberland 2 unitary authorities | No | Yes | No | Yes | No |
| N. Yorkshire unitary authority | Yes[1] | No | Yes | Yes | Yes[1] |
| Somerset unitary authority | Yes | Yes[1] | Yes | Yes[1] | No |

A  Strong, effective and accountable strategic leadership.
B  Neighbourhood flexibility and empowerment.
C  Value for money and equity on public services.
D  Affordability.
E  Supported by a cross section of partners and stakeholders.

1.  On balance or overall.

2.  In each case the decision in the July letter was 'Yes' on the Affordability criterion ('on balance' for Exeter and Ipswich). However, the proposing authorities were asked to do more work on their financial cases. All the requests included the following sentence: '*You will, therefore, be invited to undertake further work and to submit additional information on the financial viability of your proposal*'. There was no equivalent request about the Value for money criterion.

3.  The DCLG indicated the intention to refer the proposal to the Boundary Committee.

Source: DCLG letters to relevant councils, 25 July 2007.

would be five unitary counties; decisions were deferred for Bedfordshire and Cheshire; and the remaining proposals were rejected or referred to the Boundary Committee. Shortly afterwards, on 18 December, Parliament was advised that Cheshire would be divided into two unitary councils, and on 6 March 2008 it was announced that Bedford would become a unitary council, the remainder of the county also becoming a single unitary. The first of the two December announcements said that the proposals from Exeter, Ipswich and Norwich were being referred to the Boundary Committee, with the requirement that the whole of the respective counties be considered. The details of these decisions are set out in Table 2.4.

To some limited degree, there is a pattern to the outcome. With two exceptions, all of the bids that were rejected in March were for sub-unitary authorities, the exceptions being a proposal by the six Cornish districts for a unitary county and the proposal from five districts in Co. Durham for a 'pathfinder to unitary' way forward. On the other hand, the sixteen bids that went forward for consultation included unitary counties, sub-county unitary structures encompassing whole county areas, and free standing unitary cities in counties that otherwise would remain with two tier local government. Taking the July decisions and those subsequently announced in December, there were five outright county 'winners' – Cornwall, Co. Durham, Northumberland, Shropshire and Wiltshire. On the other hand, five county bids were rejected, these being Bedfordshire, Cheshire, Cumbria, North Yorkshire and Somerset. Although the DCLG accepted two unitary councils for Bedfordshire and Cheshire, the proposal for two councils covering the whole of Northumberland was rejected. Of the four city proposals, only Bedford's was accepted, the other three of being referred to the Boundary Committee, which was asked to examine the possibilities for unitary structures covering the whole of the relevant counties.

As of April 2008, there was the certainty that five counties would become unitary councils and that two other counties would be divided into two unitaries, making nine new councils in total. The smallest will be Bedford, with about 153,000 inhabitants and the largest Cornwall, approximately 524,000. At the time of writing, it was not known what the final outcome will be in Devon, Norfolk and Suffolk.

**Table 2.4**
Decisions announced to Parliament
5 and 18 December 2007 and 6 March 2008
Population 000, June 2006

*Accepted for implementation*

| | | |
|---|---|---|
| Cornwall | 524 | County unitary |
| Co. Durham | 492 | County unitary |
| Wiltshire | 450 | County unitary |
| Cheshire | 324/356 | Two unitaries for the county area |
| Northumberland | 307 | County unitary |
| Shropshire | 289 | County unitary |
| Bedfordshire | 153/241 | Two unitaries for the county area |

*No action to be taken (i.e., rejected)*

| | | |
|---|---|---|
| Bedfordshire | 393 | County unitary |
| Cheshire | 680 | County unitary |
| Cumbria | 495 | County unitary |
| Northumberland | 142/165 | Two unitaries for the county area |
| North Yorkshire | 580 | County unitary |
| Somerset | 520 | County unitary |

*To be referred to the Boundary Committee (including county areas)*

| | |
|---|---|
| Exeter | 115 |
| Ipswich | 117 |
| Norwich | 125 |

NB The main announcement was on 5 December 2007 but decisions were deferred on two proposals: Cheshire, announced on 18 December 2007; and Bedfordshire announced on 6 March 2008.

Sources: *Hansard* 5 December 2007, cols 65WS-69WS; 18 December 2007, cols 104WS-105WS; and the Explanatory Memorandum accompanying the Order to create two unitary authorities in Bedfordshire, 6 March 2008. Population figures from CIPFA 2006.

---

**Competing bids taken forward for consultation**
When sixteen bids went forward for consultation in March 2007, six of them comprised three pairs of competing bids for the relevant counties – Bedfordshire, Cheshire and Northumberland. In two cases there was a county unitary proposal vying with proposals for two unitary councils covering the whole county area; in the third case, Bedfordshire proposed

a county unitary authority, and Bedford a unitary authority with the same territory as the existing borough, with the assumption that the remainder of the county would become a second unitary authority. In itself, the idea of proposals in competition is entirely acceptable but there was an oddity about the way in which the March letters conveyed the decisions. For all sixteen proposals, the letters had the following identical wording:

> *The Secretary of State is <u>currently prepared to implement</u> the proposals that she is putting forward for stakeholder consultation if, but only if, when she comes to take final decisions she <u>remains satisfied</u> having regard to all further information received during the consultation <u>that the proposals meet</u> the criteria ...*

There was nothing in the letters about the competing bids to draw the attention of the recipients to the fact that only one of each pair could succeed. The DCLG might defend this deficiency by pointing to the need to consider 'all further information'. Because it would have been simple to include a single sentence in each of the six letters, one is left with the feeling that a standard letter had been drafted and that nobody at the Department was truly thinking about the full implications of what was being done.

## Moving the goalposts

A troubling feature of the process was the way in which the goalposts were moved, a matter to which we have already drawn attention elsewhere (Chisholm and Leach 2007). The process began during the period January-March 2007 and became public on 27 March.

At the beginning of the stage 1 evaluation process, the case officers at the DCLG were supplied with a document entitled 'Key lines of enquiry for case officers', the format and contents of which are revealing. The original 2006 criteria were set out and for each one there was a spread sheet with four columns, headed: key line of enquiry; areas of focus; assessment; risk/probability. The page dealing with the broad cross section of support faithfully reproduced the original formulation of the criterion, and the key line of enquiry was set out in the following words:

> <u>*Does the proposal have support*</u> *from a range of key partners, stakeholders and service users/citizens?*

Officers at the DCLG were being asked to assess the level of support that existed at the time proposals were submitted in January 2007, or as subsequently demonstrated in February/March. Conforming with this guidance, the first question put to Chester City Council about the proposal for two unitary councils in Cheshire, in a letter dated 9 February, read:

> *Can we just confirm why in you* [sic.] *bid you have not explained in detail whether your proposal have* [sic.] *a broad cross section of report* [sic.]?

At this stage in the process, and despite the evident literacy problems within the DCLG, officers were trying to establish whether proposals did have the requisite support before decisions were taken on whether to proceed.

On 27 March, Parliament was advised that sixteen proposals would go forward for consultation. The Written Statement from Mr Phil Woolas, then the Minister for Local Government, reproduced the original five criteria accurately, including the tests that change to future unitary structures must be Affordable and be Supported by a broad cross section of partners and stakeholders. But Mr Woolas then went on to say of the Secretary of State:

> *Her judgment is that there is at least a reasonable <u>likelihood</u> that these proposals, <u>if implemented, would achieve</u> the outcomes specified by the five criteria* (Hansard 27 March 2007, col. 72WS).

In other words, the goalposts had been shifted, particularly in respect of the level of Support. Instead of the test being Support before change would be implemented, the test had become a judgement that the Support would be forthcoming after the re-organisation. However, Members of Parliament, and everyone else, could be forgiven for reading the Statement to mean that the original tests had been applied.

Mr Woolas signalled another shift of the goalposts. As originally published, the term 'partners and stakeholders' had been amplified to include 'service users/citizens', but this wider interpretation was, for all practical purposes, jettisoned on 27 March:

> *As the Invitation explains, partners and stakeholders include all local authorities, the wider public sector, the business community, and the voluntary and community sector. It is; however, open to anyone to respond to the consultation document that we are issuing today* ... (Hansard 27 March 2007, col. 72WS).

There was no explicit mention of 'service users/citizens'. Thereby, the Government made it clear that they would not take the initiative to test public opinion, but that members of the public could write in.

Perhaps the most startling change of position with regard to the level of Support occurred during Parliament's consideration of Orders to implement new unitary councils. Speaking for the Government, Baroness Andrews said in the House of Lords:

> *Let me be clear about what the definition of 'broad cross section of support' actually means, as set out in the original invitation. It is, essentially, about whether the new unitary authority <u>genuinely meets its objectives and will work for local people</u>* (Hansard 4 March 2008, col. 1032).

When Parliament was advised in July 2007 that sixteen proposals were going forward for consultation, the proposing local authorities received individual letters notifying each one of the decision about their own bid. Those letters followed a standard structure, setting out the criteria as originally formulated and going on to say:

> *Each of those criteria specify* [sic.] *an outcome that either the change to unitary structures must achieve, or that the new unitary structures once established must deliver. Any assessment of the proposals against the criteria is, therefore, necessarily a process of judgement, reaching a view as to the likelihood of a proposal if implemented achieving the outcomes specified by each of the criteria.*

The first sentence implies that some criteria should be achieved before structural change would go forward, whereas there were others for which it would be necessary to show that a new council, once established, would achieve the relevant goals. But in the second sentence the injunction of 'must' had been replaced by the 'likelihood of a proposal if implemented achieving the outcomes specified', and, apparently, this was to apply to all five criteria. This change was confirmed by the July decision letters, in which the standard formulation was whether, in the judgement of the Secretary of State, there was:

> *A reasonable likelihood that, if implemented, the proposal would meet the outcomes specified by each of the criteria set out in the Invitation.*

Unlike the March letters, the July letters did not reproduce the criteria specified in the October 2006 invitation. Instead, DCLG arranged the

July letters in a rather curious way. Early in each letter, it was stated whether the Secretary of State judged that the proposal, if implemented, would or would not 'meet the outcomes specified by each of the criteria set out in the Invitation'. Thereafter, the letters followed a standard format, with paragraphs under headings identifying the five criteria, a format that carried two further changes to the rules of the game. First, the order of the criteria was changed. As originally set out, Affordability and stakeholder Support were listed as numbers one and two, but they were now placed in fourth and fifth position, the other three moving up the priority list. Second, the wording used to identify the criteria had been modified from the original (p.14) to that shown below:

*Strong, effective and accountable strategic leadership*

*Neighbourhood flexibility and empowerment*

*Value for money and equity on public services*

*Affordability*

*Supported by a cross section of partners and stakeholders*

The single most striking change related to the level of Support, the original wording being that a proposal: 'Must be supported by a broad cross section of partners and stakeholders'. There were less dramatic changes for the other four criteria. In effect, the July letters were structured to convey the impression that the October 2006 criteria were being applied, but the body of the letters was organised around a modified version, with the assessments framed so that they applied to the modified criteria, not the original, as may be seen from the full text about two criteria relating to the proposal for two unitary councils in Northumberland (see Chapter 3, pp. 30-31).

The next twist to the tale about the five criteria came in November 2007, with the publication by the DCLG of its assessment of the consultation responses:

*The Invitation issued in October 2006 provided that all proposals should demonstrate how they met five essential criteria …*(DCLG 2007a, para. 5).

The injunction 'must' in the original formulation had been modified to 'should'. By the time that the November document was published, the Bill had become the 2007 Act, containing Section 21, which gave retrospective authority for the actions taken by the Secretary of State before the Act commenced. These provisions applied to the invitation document issued in 2006, converting the five criteria into 'guidance as to what a proposal should seek to achieve'. Although the November document was technically correct for the time it appeared, the retrospective formulation underlines the extent to which the goalposts had been moved during the LGR. In addition, the document reproduced the five criteria in the order used in the July letters, not the order set out in October 2006, and adopted yet other variants of the wording:

> *Provide strong and accountable strategic leadership*
>
> *Deliver genuine opportunities for neighbourhood empowerment*
>
> *Deliver value for money public services*
>
> *Be supported by a broad cross-section of partners and stakeholders*
>
> *Be affordable: restructuring must represent value for money and be self-financing*

(DCLG 2007a, para. 5.)

The criteria that had become 'guidance' were presented inaccurately in a document that became relevant for Parliament when statutory Orders for implementing unitary structures were considered.

These changes in the formulation of the criteria can be explained in two mutually exclusive ways:

1.  That the draughtsman was careless and unaware that the changes carried any significance, and that those who accepted the drafting were equally careless.

2.  That the changes were deliberate, and therefore made with intent.

Whichever of these two possibilities may be correct, something was seriously amiss with the whole process. Good governance requires precision in the use of terms and consistency in their application, both of which were manifestly lacking in this case. The conclusion is inescapable: either there was sloppy drafting, or the changes were deliberate. Whichever explanation is correct, there can be no denying that the goalposts had indeed been shifted.

But then, on 5 December, Mr Healey's statement to Parliament appeared to move them back to their original position:

*The basis of these decisions is the Secretary of State's assessment of the proposals against the five criteria set out in the original invitation, and which now have the status under the 2007 Act of guidance to which councils should have had regard when making their proposals* (Hansard 5 December 2007, col. 66WS).

Immediately after this passage there followed a brief summary of the five criteria that was reasonably faithful to the original formulation, except that 'must' had been replaced by 'should':

*These five criteria are that if change is made and new unitary structures are implemented, then that change should be affordable (first criterion); and be supported by a broad cross section of partners and stakeholders (second criterion); and that the future structures should provide strong, effective and accountable leadership (third criterion); deliver genuine opportunities for neighbourhood flexibility and empowerment (fourth criterion); and deliver value for money and equity on public services (fifth criterion).*

Instead of affirming to Parliament that, in the judgement of the Secretary of State, the five criteria had been met, the 5 December statement went on to say that, having regard to all the available information:

*The Secretary of State has decided to confirm her earlier 'minded to' decisions in all cases except...*

As we have seen, the July 'minded to' letters were framed with the goalposts removed from the position set out in October 2006 but, as presented to Parliament, it appeared that the goalposts remained in their original locations, and that decisions had been reached on that basis. However, by making the decisions then announced on the basis of confirming decisions that had been taken in July, the Secretary of State was not announcing decisions on the basis of the criteria conveyed to Members of Parliament, but on the basis of the altered terms used in the July. It is difficult to arrive at any conclusion other than that Parliament was misled.

Letters to the five successful county bidders, dated 5 December, all contained the following text:

*The Secretary of State has given due consideration to the further representations received in relation to your proposal since July, and has concluded that they contain* *no new and substantive evidence to affect her decision ... I am now writing to inform you that, having had due regard to all the relevant information available, the Secretary of State has confirmed her 'minded to' decision of 25 July 2007 that there is a reasonable likelihood that, if implemented, your proposal would meet the outcomes <u>specified by each of the criteria set out in the Invitation</u>, and she accordingly intends to implement your proposal ...*

The letters implied that the criteria used in the July letters were the same as in the 2006 invitation, and that was certainly the impression conveyed to Parliament. In fact, as we have seen, the goalposts had been moved. Although the July letters each contained a prefatory reference to the criteria as set out in the invitation, they were organised under the headings of the modified criteria, each section concluding the brief discussion by saying whether the Secretary of State did or did not believe that a proposal would meet 'this criterion' or 'the criterion'. What had been decided in July was in terms of the criteria as then portrayed, not the October 2006 criteria. It is difficult to avoid the conclusion that the December letters were seeking to create the appearance that the original criteria had been met, when in fact the July letters were based on a different formulation.

## Conclusion

Our account so far has shown that the LGR process was not transparent, but opaque. As we turn to examine substantive matters in detail in the succeeding chapters, two thoughts need to be carried forward. In the first place, when we examine details of the LGR in Chapters 3, 4 and 5, we may find either that this initial pessimistic assessment of the process is misplaced, or that it is confirmed. Second, it may be that the twists and turns identified in the present chapter occurred because of the judicial review proceedings brought by Shrewsbury and Congleton, alleging that the Secretary of State had been acting unlawfully because there was no statutory provision for proceeding in the way that she chose (Chapter 6).

# 3

# Decisions under the Microscope

In accordance with the indicative timetable announced in October 2006, the DCLG issued decision letters in July 2007 on the sixteen bids that had gone forward for consultation. All the letters stated that the Secretary of State was or was not minded to proceed with the individual proposals; these were the 'minded to' letters that figured in the decisions reported to Parliament in December 2007, the Secretary of State having decided whether or not to confirm the decisions contained in the July letters. Consequently, those letters have a central place in whole LGR process. Table 2.3 records the DCLG's summary assessments for each of five criteria for each proposal. The first issue of interest is whether the July decision letters presented a coherent and consistent set of judgements? To arrive at an answer to that question, we will also draw upon the decisions for all the proposals, most of which were announced in December 2007; the conclusions for Bedford and Bedfordshire were made public in March 2008.

At one level, there is an identifiable pattern to the July decisions. For eight county unitary proposals, the respective decisions were clear-cut, the bid being either accepted (5) or rejected (3). Two county bids, Bedfordshire and Cheshire, were deemed to have passed the threshold of acceptability, but so also were competing bids that the DCLG indicated were to be preferred. Of the sub-county proposals, one was rejected, another would be referred to the Boundary Committee, and four were regarded as somewhat problematic, in that the Department wanted more work to be done on the financial cases, even though the Department was minded to implement all of them – two in preference to competing county bids. Overall, the sub-county unitary proposals were regarded as less convincing than the proposals for county unitaries, a pattern that was confirmed by the final decisions on the sixteen proposals: 50% of the county bids were ultimately accepted but only 33% of the sub-county proposals. However, matters become less clear as we inspect the detail, something that is most conveniently done in accordance with the wording of the five criteria as rendered by the DCLG in the letters written in July 2007, although we will not follow the order used in those letters.

### Affordability. Value for money and equity on public services

These two criteria overlap in substantial degree because the Affordability criterion is predicated upon the concept of Value for money, with the proviso that 'transitional costs overall must be more than offset over a period not exceeding five years'. The two criteria amount to the same thing and need to be treated together as one. This need is reinforced by the fact that comments about matters relevant for the financial assessments appeared somewhat randomly under the two headings in the July letters, and indeed under other criteria as well. For example, scale diseconomies were mentioned at least once for each of the six sub-county unitary bids, either under the Affordability criterion, or under the Value for money heading. The eight references were equally divided between the two headings, the matter being mentioned under both criteria for Exeter and Ipswich.

Somewhat odd as it may seem, a convenient starting point for this discussion is provided by the rejected bid for two unitary councils in Northumberland. There are two reasons for this choice. First, whereas the bid was rejected on grounds of Value for money, it was accepted as being Affordable. Second, the grounds given under the Value for money heading have important implications for the way other bids were evaluated. The full headings and texts for the two criteria read as follows:

#### Value for money and equity on public services
*The Secretary of State believes that the proposals will* [sic. would] *remove the confusion that currently exists about which tier of local government delivers which service. However, she is of the view that the two unitaries would in all their circumstances suffer from capacity and resource constraints that would threaten the delivery of specialist services and the ability of the authorities to react to change. She also considers there is a real risk to services – particularly the delivery of*

*county services; children's services, adult social care – as a result of the complex joint arrangements proposed in the two unitary model. She is also of the view that the proposals – if implemented would have cost implications for other public sector bodies – Fire, Police and Health, who would have to carry out some internal reorganisation to adapt to the new arrangements. Accordingly she concluded that there is not a reasonable likelihood of your proposal achieving the <u>outcomes specified by the criterion</u>.*

### Affordability
*The Secretary of State considers that the financial case looks reasonably robust and there is little risk that the proposal would be unaffordable. Accordingly she concluded that there is reasonable likelihood of your proposal achieving the <u>outcomes specified by the criterion</u>.*

Attention has already been drawn to the last four words in these texts for both of the criteria – 'outcomes specified by the criterion' - this being the standard wording employed in the July decision letters in assessing the five criteria. Although the letters contained a reference to the October 2006 formulation of the criteria, the body of the letters was structured around the re-formulated criteria, to which the term 'the criterion' must apply.

Given the negative comments and conclusion under the Value for money criterion, and given that Value for money was the prime component of the Affordability criterion, it is impossible to see how the proposal for two councils in Northumberland could be judged to be Affordable; or, alternatively, why, if Affordable, the proposal would not have given Value for money. In the starkest possible terms, the sentences quoted above for Northumberland demonstrate the muddled and contradictory thinking that lay behind the decision making on this proposal.

In a less extreme form, the same problem was evident with four proposals for unitary authorities below the county level, which were accepted on the Value for money criterion, albeit only 'overall' in two cases, but with doubts expressed about the Affordability of all four (Table 2.3). The proposers were asked to do more work on their financial cases, and it is difficult to see why that requirement did not apply to the Value for money criterion as well.

It was said of the proposal for two unitary authorities in Northumberland that they would suffer from capacity and resource constraints, which amounts to saying that they would suffer from diseconomies of scale. This same point was made for all the other sub-county unitary bids – explicitly for a unitary Bedford, for two unitaries in Cheshire and for both Exeter and Ipswich; in the case of Norwich, attention was drawn to the small population, which was another way of describing the loss of scale economies.

It was also said of the proposed two unitary councils in Northumberland that there would be 'cost implications' for the Fire, Police and Health services, presumably because of the rupture of coterminosity. The identical problem would occur with all the other sub-county proposals but the decision letters did not for any other case mention the three services identified in Northumberland. The issue was not mentioned at all in respect of unitary proposals for Bedford, Ipswich and Norwich. In the case of Exeter, it was noted under Strategic leadership that there would be some 'dilution' of coterminosity, and under this same heading it was said of two unitaries in Cheshire that the councils would 'have a broad degree of coterminosity'. It is impossible to regard these assessments as providing a coherent analysis of the realities about the impact of changes upon other agencies.

The reasons given for rejecting the two-unitary bid in Northumberland on Value for money grounds should have applied with equal force to at least four of the other five sub-county unitary bids. Nevertheless, the DCLG in July was persuaded to accept four of these proposals on this criterion ('on balance' in two cases), the fifth being Norwich, which was rejected on this criterion (see Table 2.3). The only possible basis for the DCLG coming to these conclusions seems to be contained in the July decision letter for Ipswich. Concerns were expressed by the Department about scale and capacity in terms that were fairly similar to those used for Northumberland, but those concerns were then dismissed for Ipswich with the following words, that the Secretary of State:

*Recognises that a council can enhance its capacity and take measures to overcome any skills shortage.*

The logic of this proposition is that all local authorities, whatever their circumstances, can deal with the disadvantage of small size in a fully cost effective and efficient manner. That logic was not followed elsewhere, confirming the inconsistency of the DCLG.

The inconsistency and selectivity of the DCLG was revealed with unusual clarity in the case of Bedford's unitary bid. In the July letter to the borough, the Secretary of State acknowledged concerns about children's services and adult care provision if the county arrangements were split up:

> *However, she notes that Bedford Borough are planning to work with Central Bedfordshire in the area of children's services ...*

Although the Central Bedfordshire proposal had been rejected in March, further work was done thereon, resulting in a revised submission forwarded to the DCLG in June. This document clearly described the management structure envisaged, including directors for children's services and for adult care, with no hint that services would be provided jointly with Bedford. There was no basis for the Department to offer the prospect of inter-authority collaboration in its assessment of Bedford's proposal; the Department was disingenuous.

Returning to the text quoted above for two unitary authorities in Northumberland (pp. 30-31), note the very first sentence. If the removal of confusion between the two tiers would have been beneficial in that county, why was there no reference to the matter in any of the other fifteen decision letters except for a unitary Co. Durham?

Enough has been said about Affordability and Value for money to show that there were significant inconsistencies in the evaluations given in the July 'minded to' letters. Those inconsistencies undermine confidence in the assessments made by the DCLG. Confidence is further undermined by the decisions taken for Bedfordshire and Cheshire, discussed at the end of this chapter.

### Supported by a cross section of partners and stakeholders

Initially, we will consider the three cases that the DCLG was, in July, minded to approve which were given an unqualified 'Yes' in regard to Support – Exeter, Ipswich and Wiltshire. For all three bids, the wording in the decision letter was virtually identical, so that the text for Ipswich may be cited as applying to the other two cases:

> *She* [the Secretary of State] *considers that, if implemented, the proposal would command a cross-section of support from a range of stakeholders, both public and private sector, as well as some support from the general public. She concluded that there was a reasonable likelihood of the proposal achieving the outcomes specified by this criterion.*

That is the entire text of the assessment under this heading. There was no discussion about the detail of the evidence and the quality thereof at the end of the consultation process.

In a literal sense, the terms used by the DCLG were almost certainly true, for there can be little doubt that some stakeholders and members of the public (perhaps large numbers) would come to support unitary authorities for Exeter, Ipswich and Wiltshire, were they to be established. But the terminology begs the question of how much support there would be, and ignores the issue of support for making the change before the change had been effected. The DCLG chose a form of words that technically could not be faulted within the re-defined criteria but which had little real meaning and which, in the context of the original criteria, was not relevant, because it was the proposal that needed to command a broad cross section of support before the decision was taken, not the outcome after implementation.

Different wording was used in letters about five other proposals: the two competing bids in Cheshire, and for unitary counties in Cornwall, Co. Durham and Shropshire. The text for Co. Durham is representative of this group:

> *The Secretary of State notes that of those that responded directly to the consulta-*
> *tion, there appears to be at least a reasonable level of support in most sectors. ...*
> *Whilst she recognises that the districts carried out polling which came down heavily*
> *against the proposal for a unitary council for Durham, the climate in which the*
> *polls took place, including the information that was available to voters either di-*
> *rectly or as a result of press debate suggests that the results need to be viewed with*
> *caution. On balance therefore, she concluded that there is a reasonable likelihood*
> *of the proposal achieving the outcomes specified by this criterion.*

Three features of this text stand out. First, there was no attempt to summarise the evidence that had been considered. Second, by clear implication, only responses received directly by the DCLG had been taken into account. Third, opinion polls had been discounted (even ignored?) on the basis of the 'climate' in which the polls were undertaken.

There was no suggestion that the polls themselves were badly executed and therefore no question was raised that they were to be faulted on technical professional grounds. In effect, the Department appeared to be saying that respondents had failed to arrive at the 'right' decision because the information available to them was biased against the unitary bids. It may well be that some or many respondents did come to conclusions that can be categorised as mistaken, but that is not a reason for discounting the evidence. In an electoral democracy, the Government governs on the basis of the assent accorded to it by the electorate. If the Government chooses to discount or ignore opinions that are contrary to its wishes, however irrational those opinions may be in the eyes of the Government, then this attitude undermines the basis of representative democracy.

Perhaps the most extraordinary thing is that, in assessing the rejected bid for a unitary North Yorkshire, the DCLG noted 'the polling commissioned by district councils did not show a clear outcome of *informed* opinion'. Why should the DCLG have considered public opinion in this county to be informed whereas, by implication, it was misinformed elsewhere? No explanation was offered. Is it the case that, in North Yorkshire, the polling provided an answer that the Government considered was more nearly 'right' than was the case in respect of the five bids noted above?

Matters become even less clear when two other bids are examined – a unitary Bedford city and a unitary Northumberland. The full text of the Bedford assessment read as follows:

> *The Secretary of State acknowledges the concerns raised by key stakeholders in the public sector with regard to co-terminosity and that many have said that as they currently deal only with the County Council, having to liaise with two authorities will be burdensome as they would have to manage multiple interfaces. However she also notes the support for the proposal from within Bedford, where local businesses and people see Bedford's interests being best served by a single council with all the local government levers at its control. <u>In particular she notes that almost 30,000 people have expressed a view in favour of the proposal including a petition signed by over 20,000 people.</u> She therefore concludes, on balance, that there is a reasonable likelihood of your proposal achieving the outcomes specified by this criterion.*

This was the only case in which a decision letter gave figures for the level of Support, and on this occasion the key stakeholders were over-ridden by the local businesses and members of the public within Bedford itself. There was no note of caution regarding the 'climate' in which the opinions were elicited, and no mention of the scale of opposition. Nor was there any mention of opinion in the remainder of the county area and whether a unitary Bedford would be in the best interests of residents outside Bedford. Consequently, the evidence cited was partial and might or might not accurately portray the situation. It is difficult to avoid the conclusion that data were given in this case because they happened to suit the DCLG.

These difficulties are compounded when one considers the bid for a unitary Northumberland. In this case, the support of two stakeholders was identified, the Chief of Police and the North East Chamber of Commerce. The naming of these two might imply that other stakeholders were less supportive, and highlighted the absence of equivalent detail in the other decision letters. For evidence on public opinion, the DCLG relied on a 2004 referendum, in which over 40% of respondents favoured a unitary county. However, that referendum was conducted in the context of a proposed elected regional assembly with the prospect that, were such an assembly to be established, then two tier local government would have been abolished. With that scenario in mind, the referendum asked the electorate to choose between two options for unitary local government in the county, one option being a unitary county. The results of the 2004 referendum are irrelevant to the 2007 consultation, in which the continuation of the present two-tier arrangements was a real option. It is unacceptable for the Government to respond to a consultation process by using such inappropriate material.

Only two proposals were rejected on the Support criterion, for two councils in Northumberland, and for Somerset, both of which proposals were rejected overall. The terms used in the July letters are revealing. In the case of the proposal for two unitaries in Northumberland, the text read:

> *The Secretary of State acknowledges that, whilst there is support for this proposal from a broad range of stakeholders, the proposals lack support from any key public sector stakeholders.*

It would appear that 'key public sector stakeholders' as a group effectively vetoed this proposal by withholding their support. It is not easy to reconcile this assessment with that quoted above for Bedford, and the terms set out in the original invitation to councils:

> *The Government recognise that any proposal may not carry consensus from or within all sectors. While no single council or body, or group of councils or bodies, will have a veto, it will be necessary for any proposal to have support from a range of key partners, stakeholders and service users/citizens.* (DCLG2006b, para. 3.5.)

Somerset reveals another difficulty. The July letter noted that the proposal did 'command some support' but went on to say that it:

*Would not command a sufficient broad cross-section of support from a range of stakeholders. She notes that whilst the climate in which polls were conducted suggests that the results should be viewed with some caution, there was a high turnout and a very high percentage of voters opposed to the proposal.*

Compare this formulation about opinion polls with that used elsewhere, exemplified by Co. Durham. Implicitly in Somerset, the high turnout and large percentage of 'no' votes were taken seriously by the DCLG, whereas elsewhere similar expressions of public opinion were discounted or ignored, ostensibly because of the 'climate' in which polls were conducted.

Almost no hard evidence was offered regarding the level of Support at the end of the consultation period, and the DCLG was selective in the way that the evidence or lack of it was presented, in the extreme case using irrelevant material. Opposition to proposals among members of the public was deliberately downplayed. Because the DCLG had given an undertaking that it would itself consult stakeholders and service/users/citizens, and had failed to initiate any surveys of public opinion, only one conclusion appears to be possible; Ministers were aware that many unitary proposals would be unlikely to receive public endorsement. If the public had not been persuaded, and many stakeholders as well, the fundamental conclusion to be drawn is that the case made by the proponents of change had not proved to be convincing. It appears that the Government was not willing to countenance this conclusion.

### Strong, effective and accountable strategic leadership. Neighbourhood flexibility and empowerment

The first matter to consider is the meaning of 'strategic leadership'. In normal parlance, a clear distinction is made between strategy and tactics, with strategy focussing on the broad aims, the goals to be achieved. Strategic leadership must be leadership designed to achieve clear objectives. However, the problem is that a local authority cannot act in isolation – there has to be cooperation with other local authorities, regional bodies and the national government. Strategic leadership must, therefore, mean the 'outward orientation' that is identified by the DCLG in amplifying the criterion, and related characteristics, such as:

*Strong strategic leadership*

*Take tough decisions*

*Powerful local leaders*

This description of Strategic leadership can be accepted. However, the DCLG muddled matters by including the following attributes:

*Tackling disengagement and powerlessness by shortening the distance between governors and governed*

*Personal visibility of councillors*

Both of these requirements point in the direction of Neighbourhood empowerment, not Strategic leadership, creating a significant tension between these two criteria.

Much more important is the direct conflict between the two criteria, as illustrated by the following excerpts describing Neighbourhood empowerment:

*Power and resources to influence decisions*

*Devolution of power down to local communities*

*Strong citizen focus*

*Shape service provision*

If there were to be real power at the most local level, that would place limits upon the capacity to take strategic decisions, and vice versa. To a significant extent the two criteria pull in opposite directions. If there is more of the one, there is liable to be less of the other, and for this reason they cannot be treated as independent of each other. The proper way in which to present the two criteria would be to ask for the maximisation of Strategic leadership subject to the need for Neighbourhood empowerment, or vice versa. It is impossible to maximise both simultaneously, because they are reciprocally constrained.

Consequently, the following assertions may be made with confidence. A small unitary authority, such as any of the four cities, has much more scope for empowering its citizens and neighbourhoods than a large one, primarily because there would be no reduction in the number of councillors. On the other hand, such an authority would have little real opportunity for Strategic leadership because so many issues relate to matters beyond the city's borders, requiring negotiations and compromises at numerous levels. Conversely, a large unitary authority, such as a county, would be better placed to 'punch its weight' at the regional and national levels and is therefore likely to be better placed to offer Strategic leadership than a small unitary council, but its very size would make it harder to achieve genuine Neighbourhood empowerment and citizen engagement. The basic fact is that there is a trade off between the two desirable goals.

Despite this obvious dilemma, the DCLG presented the two criteria as if they were independent, to be achieved in equal measure irrespective of the size of the proposed unitary council. As a result, the bids submitted to the Department displayed considerable contortions in trying to comply.

There is a further general point to make. Both of these criteria are fuzzy, depending upon assertions regarding what may be achieved, with very little scope for hard evidence to be marshalled. Consequently, the bid proposals went to considerable lengths to set out structures but could say little about how these might work in practice. This point is especially relevant at the regional and national levels, because partnership and cooperative working depend as much on the other agencies as upon the unitary council. But this is also true at the Neighbourhood level, which also involves other agencies, whether these be the police or voluntary bodies, etc. In a very real sense, proposals under these two criteria would have to be largely theoretical, a matter to which we return when considering some issues in Cheshire.

Given the incoherence about these two criteria, it is little surprise that the sixteen decision letters revealed muddled thinking by the DCLG. The examination that follows takes the sub-county unitary proposals first, followed by the unitary counties. In both cases, the Strategic leadership issues will be dealt with first, and Neighbourhood empowerment second.

### Sub-county unitaries: strategic leadership

The treatment of four unitary bids was remarkably similar in one important respect, it being said of Strategic leadership that, as unitary councils, they would be able to focus on their respective urban priorities. But Exeter, Ipswich and Norwich are closely circumscribed, Bedford less so. With intimate connections to their surrounding areas, the solution for perceived problems within the cities may lie outside their boundaries and therefore involve decisions by other agencies that can only be influenced, not controlled, by the cities. Second, and conversely, the surrounding areas are intimately affected by what happens in the cities, and their interests should not be ignored. These issues were not addressed. In addition, there were some odd observations by the DCLG, the relevance of which is hard to detect, as with:

> *There is alignment between the cabinet portfolios and the corporate directorates* (Bedford).

> *Enhanced scrutiny function* (Exeter and Ipswich).

> *Integrating directorates* (Norwich).

Evidently, the DCLG found it difficult to find reasons why Strategic leadership would be improved by having unitary cities.

The Secretary of State's July decisions rejected proposals for two unitary councils in Northumberland, on the grounds, inter alia, that the split between the urban and rural parts of the county are less obvious than is commonly made out, saying:

> *She notes that there are significant interactions and commuter flows between the two which mean that a high degree of strategic co-ordination and coherence is needed.*

However, these issues were not mentioned for a unitary Bedford even by implication, and only tangentially for Norwich, although the problems were recognised for Exeter and Ipswich. For the four cities, the DCLG claimed that unitary status would enable them to concentrate on 'urban priorities', which implies that the Department was willing to ignore the wider interactions.

This fundamental inconsistency of the DCLG was maintained when the decision was taken to create two unitary councils in Bedfordshire. On 6 March 2008, Bedfordshire CC received a letter containing the following passages:

> *In relation to strategic leadership, the proposal for a two-unitary Bedfordshire includes a proposal for a council led by a directly elected mayor and that the two unitaries in Bedfordshire would enable the development of sustainable community strategies and Local Area Agreements that focus on the different circumstances and priorities of Bedford and mid/ south Bedfordshire ... By allowing each of the*

*authorities respectively to concentrate on the different needs of the urban Bedford and the predominantly rural mid and south of the county ...*

Given the view taken about Northumberland, and given that, in the end, Exeter, Ipswich and Norwich were all referred to the Boundary Committee, the reasoning about the need to separate urban and rural Bedfordshire is incomprehensible. As for an elected mayor, that is not a relevant matter in considering long term structures.

### Sub-county unitaries: neighbourhood empowerment

The four proposals for unitary cities embodied few risks regarding the existing level of citizen and neighbourhood involvement, and offered the reasonable prospect that such involvement could be improved, because existing district and county functions would be handled by one council. In effect, the proposals would build on existing practices with regard to the roles of ward councillors and area committees. In the absence of reduced councillor numbers, there was every reason to expect the existing level of citizen engagement to continue. What was less certain, however, was whether there could or would be genuine empowerment, in the form of real delegation of powers and responsibilities. To the extent that such devolvement might occur, this would be within the overall limitation that the cities themselves are constrained by multiple inter-connections with their surrounding areas, whereby they could not act as free agents.

The bids for two unitary councils in both Cheshire and Northumberland were a different matter. In both cases, the DCLG expressed doubts about the precise role of the area committees/area boards, noting in the case of Northumberland the risk that they would 'lack capacity to take-on any meaningful delegation of services/decisions', and that in Cheshire 'the proposed size of electoral divisions presents a potential risk to councillors' capacity to engage with the electorate'. These concerns were reasonable given that there would be a significant reduction in the number of councillors. Nevertheless, both proposals were accepted at this stage as qualifying on the Neighbourhood empowerment criterion, unconditionally in the case of the Northumberland two-unitary bid but 'on balance' in the case of the proposal for two unitary councils in Cheshire. For the present, the key point is that the DCLG expressed concerns about Neighbourhood empowerment for both of these proposals to divide a county into two unitary authorities.

## Unitary counties: strategic leadership

We agree with the DCLG's view that, in general, a unitary county could simplify working with agencies such as Health and Police, and that strategic planning matters would probably be easier to manage. Consequently, Strategic leadership would probably be facilitated.

However, these likely benefits may be obtained by the sacrifice of benefits that arise from the existing two tier arrangements. Every county is diverse, with the consequence that the needs and aspirations of those who live in one part may not coincide with the needs and aspirations elsewhere. Serious problems may arise if the area governance arrangements in a unitary county dilute the political and administrative articulation of the geographical differentiation that exists. Unless those area governance provisions are truly robust – and consequently rather expensive – the benefits of improved Strategic leadership at the county level may well be offset, or more than offset, by the loss of representation for minority interests, the diminution of democratic accountability, and the failure to empower communities.

## Unitary counties: neighbourhood empowerment

The Government recorded concerns about the ability of the proposals for two unitary councils in Cheshire and Northumberland to achieve Neighbourhood empowerment, even though both proposals were allowed to pass on this criterion. As there were manifest grounds for concern about dividing a whole county into two unitary authorities, there should have been even greater reasons for doubting that whole counties would be able to deliver an adequate degree of devolution and empowerment. The fundamental reason is that county unitary councils would have even fewer councillors in relation to the population than would be the case if there were two authorities for the same area.

### Cornwall

A unitary county would have fewer than half the number of councillors than is currently the case when the county and district councillors are summed. The proposal for Cornwall was for a reduction from 331 to 82, the latter figure being the present number of county councillors, implying not a 50% reduction but 75%. It was on the basis of 82 councillors that the proposal was drawn up and costed by the county, although it was acknowledged that the number of councillors might have to be increased from 82 to 100. The July DCLG decision letter referred to this issue under the Strategic leadership heading with the following words, that the Secretary of State:

> *Recognises that concerns as to the viability of democratic links between councillors and their electorate appear to have been mitigated with the proposal for signifi-cantly increasing (possibly up to doubling) the current number of councillors at county level.*

 If the county really had suggested up to 164 councillors, then it is strange that the county's response (Cornwall CC 2007a) to Chisholm's critique of their case did not mention any increase in councillor numbers, so where did the Department get the idea that there might be a doubling from 82? The further point is the following. The county's financial case was based on 82 councillors. An increase above that figure would have implications for recurrent costs, and if the increase were to be anywhere near the figure hinted at by the Government, then there could well be the capital costs of a new council chamber to be taken into account.

Furthermore, when Ministerial decisions were announced in December 2007 and Orders laid, Cornwall's proposals were accepted 'without modification'. In the absence of an explicit variation in the number of councillors, the unitary county will start with 82 Members. Any change in the number thereafter will be a matter for the Boundary Committee of the Electoral Commission, and the Secretary of State has no power to direct that Committee to specify any particular number of councillors when re-warding the county. Therefore, the Government passed up its opportunity to set the number of councillors at a higher figure than 82 and has no control over the number that may eventually be determined.

The July letter about Cornwall revealed the DCLG taking shelter behind an uncosted aspiration for an increase in councillor numbers, over which they have forgone control, to mitigate the acknowledged problems that would arise for councillors interacting with their citizens, neighbourhoods and communities. The reference to a possible doubling was meaningless. Only one explanation seems to be possible: the DCLG was playing with words, and doing so in an outrageous manner.

*The general problem of area governance: real empowerment?*
County unitary authorities would have many fewer councillors than at present. Yet the greater part of constituency work falls upon district councillors, not upon their county counterparts (Wilks-Heeg and Clayton 2006). Consequently, what was the nature of the proposals put forward

by the counties to ensure that neighbourhoods and citizens would enjoy at least the same level of engagement and empowerment as at present, and preferably even more, in order to comply with the stated aims of the Government? In general terms, all the bids proposed versions of area committees, the number of areas varying from case to case, partly in response to the size and geography of the respective counties – for example, 16 in Cornwall, 20 in Wiltshire and 27 in Shropshire. How much substance did these proposals have?

Consider two county unitary bids that were rejected although passing muster on the Neighbourhood criterion, Bedfordshire and Somerset. In the former case approval was given on this criterion, although with the qualification of the word 'overall', and was given despite the fact that the Secretary of State 'considers that these arrangements involve little real delegation'. Somerset's bid was also endorsed, in this case without caveat; the DCLG's letter commented on the lack of clarity about delegation beyond the four area committees proposed, noting the Secretary of State's view that the proposals:

> *Are not clear and that the absence of meaningful devolution could be a step back-wards from the current successful local working practices in some parts of the county. She recognised, however, that clarity and devolution could readily be introduced.*

If an adequate degree of local empowerment would be possible in Bedfordshire with 'little real devolution', one has to ask why any devolution would be needed anywhere? Conversely, if 'clarity and devolution could readily be introduced' in Somerset, then the concept was fundamentally meaningless as a criterion for establishing a unitary county.

Matters become even more doubtful when one enquires about the costs associated with devolved administration within counties, costs that Table 3.1 shows to have been assessed at very low levels in several counties. In Cornwall's case, the £2.3 million p.a. identified by the county covered the additional costs to be incurred in administering the 16 areas plus small local budgets, but nothing else. Responding to Chisholm's critical assessment of the bid, the rejoinder issued by the County in June 2007 had this to say about more serious devolution:

> *If the unitary proposal is accepted, the new council would set the overall opera-tional budgets for services and their capital programmes. Depending on the service, the devolution of this budget may be considered. This will not represent an addi-*

*tional draw on the authority's budget, merely a change of the geographical scale at which decisions on priorities are taken. If this devolution takes place, it will occur within an agreed framework for measuring and monitoring both expenditure and performance to agreed targets.* (Cornwall CC 2007a, Appendix 1, para. 10.)

This passage sets out as clearly as is possible the practical constraints to proper devolution within a county area. With this in mind, it is difficult to see how the DCLG could come to the following conclusions with regard to neighbourhood empowerment in Cornwall and Shropshire:

### Cornwall
[That the sixteen community areas] *would offset the risks of the council being seen as too remote and would provide genuine opportunities for neighbourhoods to influence local service delivery and shape their local communities.*

### Shropshire
[That the 27 area committees would] *have sufficient opportunity to influence local service delivery.*

There was only one county unitary bid for which the DCLG raised no concerns about remoteness from the citizenry, Shropshire, where the sum earmarked for area governance was about £1 million, barely sufficient to pay for one full-time member of staff to service each area committee. For every other county, the issue was noted under one or other of the two criteria currently being considered, but was often brushed aside with comments along the lines used for Northumberland, where, it was said, the proposed 26 community areas would 'help ensure that the authority is not seen as being too remote'. There was a clear admission here, and for other bids accepted on this criterion in July, that the unitary counties would indeed be remote, it merely being a matter of judgement whether that remoteness would be acceptable or not.

The initial part of the DCLG's statement about the area governance proposals in Co. Durham was that they would suffice to 'reduce the risk of the authority being seen as remote from local people …', but the text continued with the words that the Secretary of State:

*Considers that the proposals provide strong 'top-down' corporate and neighbourhood governance arrangements that avoid the risk of significant duplication on the part of the council and that of its principal partners.*

**Table 3.1**

Summary data for proposed area governance:
number of areas and budgeted extra annual spending

| | Nos. areas | £ million |
|---|---|---|
| Cheshire: unitary county | 15 | 5.4[1] |
| two unitary authorities | unspecified | 6.0 |
| Cornwall | 16 | 2.3 |
| Co. Durham | 14 | 9.4 |
| Northumberland | 25 | 1.3 |
| North Yorkshire | 25 | 1.25-2.5 |
| Shropshire | 27 | 0.9 |
| Wiltshire | 20 | 0.9[2] |

1 £1.2 million for staff and £4.2 million for a contact centre.

2 No figure was included in the original submission but was provided to the DCLG in response to enquiries in February 2007.

The use of the phrase 'top down' implies little room for real local engagement, confirming what has already become abundantly clear generally.

The local governance proposals in the county unitary bids provided for little or no empowerment for neighbourhoods, or even for larger areas within the authorities. Ambitious claims were made for what would be done, but the resources identified in support of those claims were so small that the reality could not possibly meet the rhetoric. Nevertheless, the DCLG concluded that all of the county unitary bids, other than those for Cumbria and North Yorkshire, passed the area governance threshold in July. The decision letters were inconsistent, perhaps most evidently in the assertion that the defects of Somerset's proposals could readily be rectified, and the approval given for the top-down area governance proposals by Co. Durham.

## Bedfordshire and Cheshire

For these two counties, two proposals remained in contention from July – a county unitary and a sub-county proposal – and in both cases the Secretary of State indicated in July that the sub-county option was preferred. Consequently, the decision process for these two counties was different from elsewhere, for two reasons. First, a decision had to be made between the competing proposals. Second, those decisions could not be couched solely in terms of confirming July 'minded to' letters; some explanation had to be offered as to why one proposal was chosen in preference to the alternative. Because of these procedural necessities, additional light is thrown on the tangled LGR decision process.

At this juncture, we merely note that there was an important difference between the two counties for the following reason. In Cheshire, both the single unitary proposal and the alternative for two unitaries had been submitted in January 2007 and had proceeded to the consultation stage. For Bedfordshire, the matter was more complicated, in that three bids had been submitted: a county unitary authority; a unitary Bedford, with the assumption that the remainder of the county would also become a unitary council; and a separate proposal for a unitary council outside Bedford. The third proposal did not proceed to consultation in March. Therefore, in July, there was the proposal for a unitary bid, predicated on the assumption of another unitary council for the remainder of the county, but no formal proposal for this. Being minded to implement the unitary Bedford, the DCLG said in July that proposals would be invited for the remainder of the county, and such a proposal was subsequently sought and offered (see Chapter 7).

### *Prioritisation*

There were two reasons why the DCLG needed to have a procedure for comparing unitary bids. With rival bids for two counties, it was necessary to choose between the options. In addition, because the Government had set a financial envelope to limit the number of proposals to be implemented, provision had to be made to rank order proposals if the number deemed to have passed the threshold for acceptance exceeded the number permitted on financial grounds. For these two purposes, a prioritisation document was issued in June (DCLG 2007b). Although this paper was published as a consultation document, it is clear from subsequent references in Parliament to the 6 June publication that no changes were made. The procedure was only used for the first purpose, choosing between competing bids in Bedfordshire and Cheshire.

For this purpose, the document set out what appeared superficially to be a logical sequence of steps but on close inspection the procedure finessed the application of the five criteria. The first step in the paper was to replicate verbatim the five criteria as originally stated in October 2006. Then the text reproduced a paragraph from the March letters, the first sentence of which read:

> *Each of these* [five] *criteria specifies an outcome that either the change to unitary structures must achieve, or that the new unitary structures once established must deliver* (DCLG 2007b, para. 15).

Only proposals that met all five criteria could be considered.

At this point, the decision process was finessed for the comparison of competing claims, a judgement being made as to which:

> *Would be expected to deliver the long-term outcomes specified by the criteria – namely, effective strategic leadership; neighbourhood empowerment; and value for money and equity on public services – to the greater extent* (DCLG 2007b, para. 17).

With this formulation, the criteria of Affordability and Support were converted into conditions that, once fulfilled, became irrelevant. These two criteria became thresholds and it did not matter whether a proposal scraped over the bar or cleared it comfortably. The decision between rival bids would be taken on the basis of three criteria, not five. In principle, therefore, a proposal could be judged best on just two out of the five criteria originally set out, however well it might have done on the Affordability and Support criteria, neglecting the fact that performance on both these criteria could have a significant impact on the long term success of a new council.

### Bedfordshire

In July, the Secretary of State indicated that she was minded to implement Bedford's unitary proposal even though there were more doubts about it than about the county's (Table 2.3), but this indication of intent was subject to receiving a satisfactory new unitary proposal for the remainder of the county. An invitation was issued on 19 November under the 2007 Act for such a proposal to be submitted. Having received a proposal, the decision was announced on 6 March 2008 that there would be two unitary councils for Bedfordshire – Bedford and the remainder of the county. Writing to the county council, the DCLG said the Secretary of State judged the two unitary proposal to be better than a single council on all three of the criteria noted above for prioritisation, including Value for money, saying:

> *On balance ... the proposal for a unitary Bedford would deliver to a greater extent the long-term outcomes specified by the criteria around strategic leadership, neighbourhood empowerment and value for money and equity on public services. ... Although the single unitary proposal might have the potential to achieve to a greater extent* [than a single council] *the criterion on value for money and equity on public services, this judgement needs to be balanced against the judgements she has reached on the other two criteria, where her judgement remains that the single authority would deliver less effective strategic leadership and community and neighbourhood empowerment. Accordingly, she has concluded that in the round a two-unitary Bedfordshire is reasonably likely to deliver to the greater extent the outcomes sought in the three criteria.*

There was a direct contradiction about Value for money. The first reference implied that two unitary councils would perform better on the criterion of Value for money but the letter made it clear that a single authority would outperform the two. Consequently, Bedford's proposal was deemed superior on just two out of the five criteria originally set out.

It would seem that Bedford's mayor was right in his comment about the March 2008 decision:

> *It's clear the Government has backed our proposals all along, despite comments made by the county council (Municipal Journal* 13 March 2008, p. 1).

### Cheshire

As with Bedfordshire in July, Cheshire CC's single unitary bid was judged to perform better across the five criteria than would two unitary councils (Table 2.3). Using the same prioritisation procedure, the decision was then reduced to the same three criteria as in Bedfordshire's case, with the same initial statement in the 18 December letter that the two unitary proposal performed better on all three. However, there were also some significant differences between the reasons given for preferring two councils.

In July, rather similar words had been used for the area governance arrangements proposed in the competing Cheshire bids. It was then thought that the county's bid offered the prospect of 'strong neighbourhood engagement', and that the two-unitary option provided 'a powerful role for area committees'. In both cases, however, the positive assessment was tempered by an identical phrase expressing concern that there was 'a potential risk to councillors' capacity to engage with the electorate' on account of the large electoral divisions proposed. Those assessments should be compared with what was said about area governance in the letters issued on 18 December 2007. First, in respect of the rejected county bid:

> [The Secretary of State] *accepts that what is proposed is imaginative and interesting but considers that these <u>proposals are largely theoretical</u>. She notes that this contrasts with the proposed neighbourhood arrangements in the two unitary option, which builds on current experience developed by district councils on the ground, in particular drawing on best practice in model arrangements used in Chester.*

As for the successful two-unitary bid, the relevant passage read:

> *As to reaching a judgement between the two Cheshire proposals, in July the Secretary of State took the view that a <u>single unitary authority would be too big</u> and there were risks that the authority would be seen as remote by local people and hence <u>less able to deliver neighbourhood empowerment</u>.*

For the DCLG to dismiss the county's localisation proposals on the grounds of being 'largely theoretical' was curious. The county had set out proposals that were as detailed as the most thorough proposals from any other county. If the county's proposals in Cheshire were theoretical, the same was true of all the other county proposals, including those of the five counties that were ultimately successful in their bids. In addition, recollect that Somerset's bid lacked clarity but that the DCLG considered that 'clarity and devolution could readily be introduced'. The stated judgement about area governance in a unitary Cheshire was seriously inconsistent with the judgements reached on the other county bids. Furthermore, the proposal for two authorities in the county was vague concerning the details of area governance, beyond building upon existing good practice in Chester. If the county's proposals for area governance were 'theoretical', then so too were those for two councils. The DCLG's reason for preferring the two councils on this criterion was specious.

As for a single unitary council in Cheshire having been deemed 'too big' in July, the letters sent that month to the competing authorities contained no statement to this effect. The nearest that the DCLG came to saying this of the county was the identical phrase that was used for the two unitary councils, raising concerns about the potential risk that councillors would not be able to engage with the public. On the area governance criterion, the July assessment was that the proposal for two unitaries achieved the threshold of acceptability 'on balance', whereas there was no such hesitation over the county's case (Table 2.3). The December letter contained a statement about the July letters that was not true.

However, the most troubling feature of the decisions relating to Cheshire is the same as the one described for Bedfordshire. Mr Healey's Written Statement to Parliament on 18 December contained the following passage:

> *Overall, she* [the Secretary of State] *has decided that it is more likely that the long-term outcomes around strategic leadership, neighbourhood empowerment and <u>value for money and equity on public services</u> would be delivered to the greater extent by the proposal for a two unitary Cheshire* (*Hansard* 18 December 2007, col. 104WS).

That assessment was replicated in the first part of the letter sent to Chester and supporting local authorities in the county, the part thereof leading up to the decision to proceed with the option for two unitaries. Thereafter, the Cheshire letter contradicted the Value for money assessment, and did so in substantially more emphatic terms than were employed for Bedfordshire. So that there should be no misunderstanding, the first part of the relevant paragraph is reproduced:

> *In relation to <u>value for money and equity on public services</u>, the Secretary of State, having regard to all the information and evidence now available, continues to accept that the potential economies of scale would be larger for a county unitary. She notes, however, that the two-unitary option opens up the possibility for new innovative ways of working, such as the proposals for operating a joint Children's Trust, although she is aware that questions have been raised about the merits of such a trust. She has concluded that, on balance, a single Cheshire unitary would*

*be reasonably likely to achieve to a greater extent* [than two unitaries] *the out-comes specified by this criterion, from the consultation document, Means of Prioritising Proposals.*

As in Bedfordshire, the decision reached between competing bids was on the basis that Affordability and Support were not relevant, and that the two unitary proposals scored better on two out of the three remaining criteria. It is impossible to regard these decisions as anything other than the artefact of a procedure designed to yield an outcome that had been determined long before the 2007 Act commenced.

## Conclusion

The preceding discussion has revealed what appears to be a close parallel with a difficulty experienced by the House of Lords Select Committee on Relations between Central and Local Government (SCRCLG 1996, para. 5.17, fn). The Committee had received evidence from the Treasury and jointly from Chisholm and Mr Derek Thomas, sometime chief executive of Surrey CC, about local government finance and, finding it impossible to accept the Treasury's argument about macro-economic matters, quoted the final sentence of the following passage from Lewis Carroll's *Through the Looking Glass*:

> 'There's glory for you!' 'I don't know what you mean by "glory"', Alice said. 'I meant, "there's a nice knock-down argument for you!"' 'But "glory" doesn't mean "a nice knock-down argument"', Alice objected. 'When I use a word,' Humpty Dumpty said in a rather scornful tone, 'it means just what I choose it to mean, — neither more nor less.'

# 4

# Dodgy data

When Parliament was advised that five counties would become unitary councils, Mr Healey said:

> *On the basis of councils' current estimates, the savings from these five proposals, once implemented, will be over £75 million annually, giving councils opportunities for improved services or lower council taxes* (*Hansard* 5 December 2007, col. 67WS).

There was no reference to the costs that would be incurred to make the transition. Using councils' own figures as at June 2007, the collective cost of transition would be £77 million, but there are very good grounds for believing that neither figure was realistic.

Mr Healey omitted to tell Parliament that the figure of 'over £75 million' annual savings was made up of the gross savings estimated by four of the counties; the only county figure for recurrent savings that was in some degree net was Northumberland's. Because there would be some additional on-going costs that would, to some extent, offset the gross savings, the sum available 'for improved services or lower council taxes' would be less than stated. On this matter, Parliament was misled.

Some idea of the scale of the problem arising from the use of gross instead of net figures may be illustrated in the following way. Each of the counties provided figures for the cost of the proposed area governance arrangements, costs that Northumberland netted out from their gross savings in presenting their headline figure for savings. If one takes the self-assessed costs of area governance for the remaining four counties, these came to £13.5 million, a figure that ought to be deducted from the gross savings. In addition, not one of the five counties showed an offset for pay harmonisation, which can be conservatively estimated at £0.5 million for each county area, or £2.5 million p.a. in total (see p. 74), and Shropshire identified an annual sum of £2.5 million for 'service reinvestment'. In other words, taking the self-assessed cost of area governance and Shropshire's 'service reinvestment' at face value, plus pay harmonisation, nearly £20 million p.a. should have been deducted from the gross figure, to give an aggregate net annual saving of about £55 million. But, as we shall see, that would be just the beginning.

Note also Mr Healey's reference to councils' current estimates, which carries the clear implication that the DCLG had accepted the councils' own self-assessments, but without actually saying so. There was no explicit statement to Parliament that the aggregate figure given represented the Government's own estimate based upon all the information that had been received, although in parliamentary debates there was mention of independent consultants having been used by the Department.

Was the Government justified in offering the figure of over £75 million as the (gross) sum that would be saved annually from the creation of five county unitary authorities? To answer this question, we need first to consider whether the self-assessments changed from their original estimates in response to questions raised by the DCLG and as result of the consultation period that ended in June 2007. Second, we need then to see whether the assessments were soundly based.

There are two preliminary tests that can be applied. When Parliament was advised in July that nine proposals that were going forward for implementation, it was said that they would result in a collective annual saving exceeding £150 million. Table 4.1 records the self-assessed figures for eight of the those proposals but not for Ipswich (£15.3 million); the total self-assessed savings recorded was £156.9 million, a figure consistent with that given to Parliament. On this test, it is clear that in July the DCLG had accepted the self-assessed estimates for recurrent savings put forward by the proposers of unitary structures.

A test in the identical form can be applied to the figure of over £75 million given for the five counties in December. At the beginning of the consultation period, the sum of the headline figures for annual savings provided by the county councils stood at £78.0 million, and had barely changed by June, then being £78.3 million. On the figures given to Parliament during the consideration of the Orders to implement structural changes, the annual savings had crept up to £80.0 million. For all

## Table 4.1
### Headline cost and saving figures for unitary councils, January and June 2007, and 2008

£ million

| | | Transition Costs[1] | | | Annual Saving[2] | | |
|---|---|---|---|---|---|---|---|
| | | January | June | 2008[3] | January | June | 2008[3] |
| Bedfordshire: | 1 unitary | 16.9 | 16.9 | | 26.6 gross | 26.6 | |
| | 2 unitaries[4] | 27.0 | 27.9 | 35.9 | 20.3 gross | 21.3 gross | 18.7 |
| Cheshire: | 1 unitary | 21.1 | 21.1 | | 21.4 net | 21.4 | |
| | 2 unitaries[4] | 14.1 | 16.6 | 25.0 | 19.8 gross | 30.1 gross | |
| | | | | | 16.3 net | 24.1 net | 16.0 |
| Cornwall | | 19.3 | 19.0 | | 17.7 gross | 17.0 | 15.0 |
| Co. Durham | | 12.4 | 12.0 | | 20.5 gross | 21.0 | 21.0[5] |
| Cumbria | | 21.3 | 21.3 | | 22.2 gross | 22.2 | |
| Exeter: | Exeter | 6.5 | - | | 11.9 gross | - | |
| | Devon | ? | - | | 1.4[6] gross | - | |
| Northumberland | | 18.0 | 18.0 | | 17.0 net | 17.4 | 17.0 |
| N. Yorkshire | | 13.5 | 13.5 | | 14.0 gross | 14.0 | |
| Shropshire | | 5.0[1] | 9.8 | | 7.8 gross | 7.9 | |
| | | 9.7[1] | | | | | |
| Somerset | | 12.0 | 12.0 | | 25.5 net | - | |
| | | | | | 27.2 gross | 27.2 | |
| Wiltshire | | 18.0 | 17.9 | | 15.0 gross | 15.0 | 18.0 |

1. Transition costs are shown on the basis that the gross cost equals the net cost. Shropshire originally showed transition costs net at about £3 million, revising this to £5.2 gross for the January submission then to £9.7 million in February. See text.

2. Figures shown net are on the basis of headline figures given in the bid documents, which may or may not be the appropriate degree of adjustment from the gross figures. All the June figures for counties have been taken from PWC (2007). PWC did not specify gross or net but it is evident that the figures are for gross savings, except for Cheshire CC, where they used the net figure.

3. Figures provided by the Government to Parliament. In the case of recurrent savings, not specified whether net or gross but the inference is gross except for two unitaries in Cheshire.

4. The proposal for a unitary Bedford assumed a unitary outcome for the remainder of the county and the financial case was prepared on that basis. The 2008 figures are the ones accepted by the Government following a new submission by the two districts in the remainder of the county in response to an invitation issued in November 2007.

5. *Hansard* records Baroness Andrews as giving a figure of £11 million for Co. Durham but simple arithmetic shows that she must have intended to quote £21 million.

6. According to the Exeter bid, this sum would be 'available to finance service developments and any transitional cost' for the county.

NB The bids listed in this table are those for which Chisholm examined the financial cases submitted by the bidders, plus Bedfordshire, Cumbria and Northumberland. The 2008 figures are late 2007 or 2008. None of the figures has been discounted to Present Value.

Sources: January 2007 bid documents and supplementary information; PWC 2007, 14 June figures for county bids; *Hansard* 21 February 2008, cols GC 23-64; *Hansard* 26 February 2008, col. 106; Explanatory Memorandum for the Bedfordshire structural change Order 2008.

---

practical purposes, the DCLG had accepted the figures put to them by the proposing counties, which implies either that those estimates proved to be remarkably robust, or that the DCLG was not very thorough in its examination of the financial cases put forward.

The proposal for two unitary councils in Cheshire provides some odd information. As Table 4.1 shows, the gross annual savings claimed in June amounted to £30.1 million, whereas the figure given by the Government in February 2008 was £16 million, virtually the same as the net figure of £16.3 million originally given in support of this bid. It seems extraordinary that the DCLG was willing to countenance the £30 million savings in July, only to adopt a figure half that six months later; no explanation has been offered. Less remarkable changes also occurred in assessing the proposal for two unitary councils in Bedfordshire.

At this preliminary level, it is reasonable to suppose that the DCLG was not rigorous in the way that the financial cases were assessed, an inference that is reinforced by the discussion that follows.

## Only marginal changes to estimates of savings

Table 4.1 records data for the nine bids examined by Chisholm plus three additional counties, so that all the county unitary bids are included in the table, thereby enabling a comparison for the ten county proposals between the headline figures in January in June. The June figures were taken from the local authority websites on 14 June (PWC 2007). Six of the counties had not changed their over-all estimates for annual savings and the largest adjustment among the remaining four counties was Cornwall's downward revision of £0.7 million. Therefore, very near the end of the consultation period, the counties were either standing firm on their original figures or had made only small and essentially insignificant changes; the net change for the five counties that were singled out for unitary status in July was an upward adjustment from £78.0 million to £78.3 million p.a. Three cases illustrate the unwillingness of those putting forward bids to respond to criticisms of their financial cases by making significant adjustments, as set out below.

Chisholm was commissioned by some of the districts in Cornwall to evaluate the county's bid documents, completing the task on 10 May. His report identified the costings that seemed reasonable, and likewise discussed those for which there were good reasons for believing that they erred. Less than a month later, on 4 June, the county issued a press release that included the following comment, that their figures 'are supported by independent financial consultants'.

At about the same time, an undated document was released by the county, the purpose of which was to rebut criticisms. In this rebuttal document, the following passage appeared, reiterating the originally estimated annual saving of £17.7 million:

> *In the absence of any reasonable criticism by Chisholm, and following the verification of the figures included in OneCornwall/OneCouncil by PriceWaterhouse-Coopers, the stated gross annual saving of £17.7m continues to represent a robust and conservative valuation of the savings that unitary status would deliver* (Cornwall CC 2007a, para. 16).

Cheshire CC issued a rebuttal in June of the critical appraisal that had previously been prepared by Leach and Chisholm. The county summarised its own January document, with the assertion that the original estimates stood:

*In order to check both the affordability of this investment* [transition costs] *and to assess how exactly the £21.4m* [of savings] *would be delivered, our figures were checked against a local model. This indicated savings of £28.4m (£23m after taking account of new localism costs). Our prudent approach claims only the lower saving of £21.4m rather than £23m in our financial appraisal. The County Council therefore remains confident that the overall level of savings predicted is cautious, robust and deliverable.* (Cheshire CC 2007a, p. 10.)

Responding to another Cheshire CC document (Cheshire CC 2007b), the districts favouring two unitary authorities in the county had this to say:

*We also again draw your attention to the County Council's attempts to undermine our financial case; there is no justification for this. We would ask you* [the DCLG] *to satisfy yourselves that our financial case is robust based on our proposals and our business case.* (Cheshire JDC 2007a, para. 3.)

But these authorities went much further than that, because the original submission was overtaken by revised figures at the end of the consultation period. Although their website on 14 June continued to show the cost and saving figures submitted in the January proposal, these data had been replaced by a submission at the end of the consultation period (Cheshire JDC 2007b). Transition costs had been increased by £2.5 million, to £16.6 million, and gross annual savings by £10.3 million to £30.1 million, figures that suggest a policy of attack being the best means of defence, and the belief that the DCLG would accept the revised figures.

In all three cases, the proposing authorities were refusing to accept any adverse criticism of their estimates, and in one case there was a substantial increase in the value of estimated annual savings. Taking this evidence in conjunction with the information in Table 4.1, it is clear that, in general, the proponents of change were not prepared to countenance any significant downward change to their estimates for on-going savings should their proposed unitary authorities be established. This indisputable fact may be interpreted in one of two ways. First, it may indeed be the case that all of the criticisms, from whatever quarter, were misplaced and therefore to be ignored. Alternatively, the DCLG itself had been so superficial in its probing of the proposals that the bidding authorities saw no reason to amend their figures in any substantial way. In order to explore these two possibilities, it is necessary to turn to some detailed examination of the questions posed by the DCLG in respect of the bids received, and the financial details contained in the bid documents.

## How probing was the DCLG?

Having received twenty-six bids in January 2007, the DCLG wrote in February to councils with queries about the proposals. The letters sent to the sixteen bidders whose proposals went forward for consultation display several characteristics relevant for our discussion. Many of the questions concerned issues such as the manner in which strategic leadership would be exercised and how devolved governance proposals would work in practice. Questions of this kind may be termed 'soft', about imprecise concepts, issues that could be no more than statements of intent, and therefore giving plenty of scope for long and essentially meaningless answers. Comparatively few questions were asked about the 'hard' data contained in the financial estimates, questions for which reasonably precise answers could be expected.

No challenge was offered to the use of gross annual savings instead of net savings. With very limited exceptions, the DCLG did not point out that some items either of cost or saving had been omitted from the tallies. In addition, although bids contained significant individual items that were difficult to justify, the Department showed no inclination to press the proposing authorities on such matters. From the way in which the letters were constructed, it is clear that each proposal was considered in isolation. No attempt was made in the February letters to make comparisons across the bids, comparisons that undoubtedly would have raised some queries in the minds of officials.

Initially, two case studies will be presented to illustrate the general points that have been made above, the examples being the unitary bid by Exeter and the proposal for two unitary authorities in Cheshire. Thereafter, we will discuss some specific problems contained in other proposals.

### Exeter

The material for Exeter's unitary bid provides a convenient starting point for our enquiry. Table 4.2 reproduces the questions that were posed, of which it is numbers six to nine that are relevant in the context of the financial appraisal. To understand whether these questions were or were not probing, it is necessary to understand some of the details contained in the bid document. Over the five year period prescribed by the DCLG for the financial analysis, Exeter claimed that there would be an aggregate of £51.6 million savings on becoming a unitary council. About two fifths of this sum (£20 million) were accounted for by annual savings of £4 million which were described as 'excess' expenditure, a figure that had been calculated in the following manner. Rita Hale Associates were asked two reasonable questions, and supplied answers, with suitable caveats. The first question was: what did the formulae used by central government indicate as the level of local authority spending in a unitary city? Second, how much was the county currently spending in Exeter, expenditure that could be added to the district's own spending to give a total for actual annual outlays? The result of this exercise showed that current expenditure in Exeter was £4 million p.a. greater than the formulae indicated, and the bid document treated this £4 million as 'excess' spending, showing this figure as an annual saving from vesting day. This procedure ignored the existence in Exeter of a County Record Office and a central library, plus three schools that cater for children with special needs. These and other services are available for Exeter's citizens and for citizens across the county, or even beyond. To treat the figure as a saving implies that facilities would cease to exist. In practice, it is reasonable to assume that the relevant facilities would remain and therefore, if not paid for by Exeter citizens, would have to be funded by the county. But Exeter's assessment of the financial impact on the county's finances of making the city a unitary authority did not mention the £4 million, which, in one form or another, would be an ongoing commitment. In other words, two fifths of the headline figure for aggregate savings over five years for a unitary Exeter were fictitious.

The second major problem with Exeter's figuring was the following. Appendix 18 to the bid document set out figures, including the claimed annual saving of £51.6 million already mentioned: on the council's own estimation, this tabulation showed cumulative savings of only £12 million over the five year period after transition costs of £6.5 million had been repaid. On the information provided, even that figure was doubtful, because the aggregate additional costs over five years were shown to total £30 million for the following headings:

- In-year re-structuring
- Service developments
- Financing costs
- Transfers from reserves

## Table 4.2
Questions put to Exeter by the DCLG in a letter dated
12 February 2007

1. Can you clarify the expected number of executive members for the new council and their respective roles and responsibilities?

2. Could you explain in greater detail how the committee structure will work?

3. How will the Council's corporate structure deliver cross-cutting strategic capacity?

4. Could you provide more detail on the plans to declare Exeter a Zero Waste city? What does this mean in practice and how will this be achieved?

5. Can you explain how, through the structural arrangements that you are putting in place, local people will influence the decisions of the executive?

6. It would be helpful to us to understand in more detail the plans for commissioning certain services from providers.

7. We note that you anticipate incurring some £4.4 million capital expenditure during transition, which will be funded by borrowing in the usual manner. It is not clear from the table on page 78 of the proposal which cost elements contribute to this figure. (The addition of IT and Accommodation costs totals some £3.4m.) Can you help?

8. More generally, it would be helpful if you could outline your current capital spending plans (or point to where this may be already have been provided in the document).

9. It would also be useful to know the extent to which your financial analysis has considered the implications of having to harmonise pay arrangements across a unified workforce.

NB The text reproduced above retains the original wording and order of the questions, and therefore the incorrect use of the Indicative Mood instead of the Subjunctive Mood.

---

The further oddity about Exeter's bid was the manner in which the impact on the county was assessed. Despite the claim that the county's transition costs had been recognised, no figure was provided, and the county was credited with a small annual saving, somewhat in excess of

£1 million p.a.. That is to say, by disaggregating the county's services, Exeter sought to show that both the county and the city would benefit financially.

In the light of this brief discussion, it is clear that the four financial questions posed by the DCLG in February failed to address fundamental issues in the financial case, concentrating instead on peripheral matters and, in one case, a question that was irrelevant – the query about the current capital spending plans of Exeter as a district. By no stretch of the imagination was Exeter's financial case subjected to probing examination at the beginning of the LGR process. Nevertheless, the DCLG did ultimately conclude that the financial case had not been made:

> *Allowing a reasonable estimate for costs, the pay back period for your proposal may be over the 5 years specified by the affordability criterion* (letter to Exeter, 5 December 2007).

That Exeter had failed to provide a robust financial case should have been obvious in March 2007.

### Cheshire: two unitary authorities

When the DCLG wrote on 9 February 2007 to raise a number of questions about the proposal for two unitary councils in Cheshire, concern was expressed that savings had been included which should have been excluded, specifically, savings arising from the programme initiated by the county council and known as 'Transforming Cheshire'. A figure of £6.5 million in annual savings had been identified as originating from this source, about one third of the £19.8 million claimed as the total gross saving. These savings were related to customer access, shared services, ICT and service efficiencies. Despite having noticed the erroneous inclusion of £6.5 million in the claimed savings, the fact that the proposers of this option increased the assessed gross annual savings to £30.1 million at the end of the consultation period indicates that there cannot have been any serious follow-up by the DCLG. Indeed, when Mr Healey claimed in July that nine unitary proposals would collectively save at least £150 million p.a., that figure must have included £30 million for the proposed two councils in Cheshire, even though the DCLG asked for further work to be done on the financial case. This indicates at least provisional acceptance of the figure at that stage of the LGR.

During September and October, the DCLG posed several questions about the financial case for two Cheshire unitary councils but did not directly query the sharp increase in estimated annual savings. Indeed, the DCLG was told:

> *The gross savings identified in the spreadsheet workbooks submitted in October are 'remarkably close' to the figures in the June submission because they are one and the same. The reason there is a difference of £0.1 million is due to a rounding difference from completing a worksheet for the East and the West.* (Cheshire JDC 2007c, para. 4.5.)

With these words, the Cheshire districts showed that they felt they had nothing to fear from enquiries by the DCLG, and that they believed their figures would be accepted. In the event, the Department ultimately accepted substantially lower recurrent savings and higher transition costs than had been estimated by those proposing two authorities in Cheshire (Table 4.1).

There are two troubling matters arising from this change of mind. When the Order was laid before Parliament to implement the structural change, the accompanying Explanatory Memorandum (para. 8.2) stated that the revised costings had been 'estimated by the proposing authorities', a statement that was not true and was contradicted by Mr Healey when the House of Commons debated the Order (*Hansard* 26 February 2008, cols 1045 and 1062). The information presented to Parliament was contradictory, a matter of some importance for the functioning of the legislature. Second, as of June 2007 and into the autumn, the DCLG had evidently been willing to accept the much more optimistic figures proposed by the bidders, only at the last minute realising that they were unacceptable. This confirms that through much of the LGR the DCLG had not been scrutinising the financial cases with much rigour.

### Curious assessments of costs and savings

The discussion which follows shows that the superficial questioning by the DCLG was not confined to the bids by Exeter and for two unitary councils in Cheshire, and that it applied as much to transition costs as to recurrent savings. In general terms, items of transition costs were omitted and others seriously under-estimated, and there were under-estimates of recurrent offsetting costs and over-estimates of savings, issues that were not adequately identified by the DCLG. These propositions will be illustrated by specific examples.

## Table 4.3
### Transition costs
### Items omitted from bidders' headline cost estimates

| | |
|---|---|
| Pension costs not explicitly identified | Somerset, Wiltshire |
| Staff recruitment and/or relocation | Cornwall, Co. Durham, North Yorkshire Somerset |
| IT | Cheshire(×2)[1], Northumberland, Shropshire[2] |
| Interest cost on borrowing/use of reserves | Cheshire (×1), Cheshire (×2), Cornwall, Co. Durham, Exeter, North Yorkshire, Shropshire |
| Legal costs | Cheshire (×2), Cornwall, Shropshire |
| Rebranding/corporate image | Cheshire (×2), Cornwall, Somerset |
| Premises costs, other than workstations | Cheshire (×2), Cornwall, N. Yorkshire, Shropshire[3], Somerset |
| County's transition costs | Exeter[4] |

1.  Cheshire CC estimated IT transition costs for a unitary county. It is inconceivable that there would be zero costs for two unitaries  - see text.

2.  Shropshire included a total of £0.7 million for IT transition costs but this was made up of recurrent spending that was already budgeted, covering only the replacement of personal computers and an IT customer service centre.

3.  Shropshire included £0.7 million over five years for a customer service centre, being funding that had already been budgeted.

4.  See text.

NB   Shadow council costs and the grants to councils for the cost of being in business have been excluded from this table because of the confusion regarding their inclusion/exclusion – see text. Practice about inclusion or exclusion varied from one bid to another.

## Transition costs

As Table 4.3 shows, three proposals entered a zero cost for the investment needed to harmonise the IT systems necessary for bringing county
and district functions together, the three cases being the proposal for two
unitary councils in Cheshire, and for unitary authorities in Northumberland and Shropshire. Other counties proposed unrealistically low costs.

Co. Durham included a figure of £0.5 million for 'IT and property', a
sum so inadequate that it is difficult to understand how it was put
forward. North Yorkshire estimated the transition costs for IT at £1.4
million but, on the admission of the chief executive, this figure, and the
transition costs in general (at £13.5 million), would have been sufficient
only for 'the early changes', and the 'two big costs are IT and staff
redundancy' (*Harrogate Advertiser,* 9 February 2007).

Even the £3.8 million budgeted by Cornwall CC for IT costs on becoming a unitary council would, on their own admission, suffice only for
what was called a 'tactical fix' before vesting day. On their figures, there
would be a further £1 million thereafter for what was labelled the
'strategic fix'. Whether the latter would be sufficient is not material in the
present context; Cornwall explicitly under-stated the transitional IT
liabilities in their figure for the transition costs of structural reorganisation. As with the other IT problems identified above, the DCLG allowed
Cornwall's under-estimate to go unchallenged.

Co. Durham presents an interesting problem about the scale of job
losses and hence the aggregate cost of staff severance. A sum of £6.7
million was identified for severance costs relating to a reduction of 139 in
the number of posts. For a county the size of Co. Durham, 139 was a
very low rate of job loss in comparison with other county proposals, e.g.,
Shropshire, where 183 posts would be shed, according to the county's
figures. For Co. Durham, a figure of at least 250 would seem to be
appropriate on the basis of comparisons with other bids. Looking ahead
to the discussion of recurrent savings, the county identified annual
economies of £6.5 million over and above the savings that were explicitly
tabulated in relation to the 139 posts. Virtually the whole of this additional saving of £6.5 million could only come from job losses in excess
of the admitted number, this implying an excess somewhat over 100 in
total. The implication is clear, £6.5 million p.a. of savings was claimed
without recording the associated severance costs. Thereby, the aggregate
transition cost was under-stated by several million pounds; or annual
savings were exaggerated. The DCLG did not identify this difficulty.

### *Exaggerated recurrent savings*

Two counties, Cornwall and Co. Durham, included substantial items for recurrent savings that are impossible to justify, for reasons that will take a bit of explaining, but were not challenged by the DCLG.

#### *Cornwall*

Cornwall used three methodologies to provide checks on their basic costing of annual savings, these broadly confirming the magnitude that had been estimated for savings in support and corporate services, i.e., the central 'overheads' involved in administering local government. They also deployed a fourth approach to provide an estimate of additional savings on frontline services. The sole description of this fourth estimation procedure in the bid document was the following statement:

> *Method 4 – a review of statistical information available on services for the Districts of Cornwall. This analysis examined what cost savings may be achieved if under a unified council, performance for district services could be improved to either the average or the highest performance currently being achieved within Cornwall (performance being judged by cost per head).* (Cornwall CC 2007b, p.73.)

If the cost per head for each service in each district were brought to the average cost per head, then the saving would be £6 million p.a.; if the cost reductions were to the lowest district cost for each service, then the saving would be £11 million p.a. The county adopted the figure of £6 million, and included this figure as part of the aggregate saving that they estimated.

This desk exercise ignored a number of fundamental matters. The implicit assumption is that differences in expenditure per head reflect differences in administrative efficiency and nothing else, an assumption that is not tenable. The need for coastal defences and flood control varies with the local geography; homelessness and the needs that this occasions are spatially concentrated; and the merit of locally elected councillors is supposed to be, inter alia, that decisions can be taken which reflect local priorities that may be deemed to be 'political' in the non-party political sense. There was no discussion in the Cornish submission as to how the district services would be altered to achieve the saving of £6 million p.a., even though the sum represented about one third of the headline savings claimed by the county. Given the hypothetical nature of the saving, it had no place in a business plan for a unitary county, but the DCLG did not raise any query about this figure in February 2007.

## Co. Durham

Co. Durham presented a very similar problem, a problem that has already been touched upon in the discussion of transition costs – the £6.5 million p.a. of savings over and above the savings linked to the identified job losses. The county claimed that £15.6 million p.a. would be saved on corporate and central services. This figure compares with the total for the county council and the districts shown by the Chartered Institute of Public Finance and Accountancy for 2006/07 amounting to £22.6 million, excluding Member allowances (CIPFA 2006). Of this total, the districts accounted for £17.5 million and the county for £5.0 million. The county's claim, therefore, was that the entire central costs of work done by the districts could be undertaken for just £1.9 million.

So how did the county estimate the savings stated? Several individual headings were specifically itemised by the county, such as the reduction in salary costs arising from the reduced number of chief executives; collectively, these itemised savings accounted for all 139 posts to be shed, and summed to £9.1 million. The additional saving of £6.5 million was attributed to a 'new model' of service delivery for corporate services, the nature of which was not described but can be inferred from the documentation provided by the county. According to the CIPFA data, the county's central administration costs amounted to 1.9% of total spending other than the ring fenced budget for schools. District expenditure, other than housing benefits, amounted to £94 million in 2006/07. If district services central costs were just 1.9%, the same as the county's percentage, then central costs for the services provided by the districts would amount to £1.8 million. If this sum is deducted from the CIPFA total for district central costs (£17.5 million) one gets £15.7 million as the sum to be saved, a figure that, with rounding errors, is identical to the aggregate saving claimed by the county, £15.6 million. The 'new model' saving of £6.5 million is the difference between the figure of £15.6 million and the itemised savings amounting to £9.1 million, and is based on some very simple arithmetic that hardly qualifies as a 'new model' but evidently the DCLG was willing to accept this component of the estimated annual savings.

This desk exercise incorporated numerous assumptions that are no more plausible than those employed by Cornwall. The fundamental issue in the Durham context, and indeed elsewhere, is whether the accountancy conventions employed by districts and counties are or are not the same, and therefore whether the CIPFA data reveal different levels of administrative efficiency or whether they are artefacts of differing circumstances. The clear presumption has to favour the latter possibility. Large organisations are able to assign central overheads to major service divisions in a way that is not possible with smaller ones, with the implication that recorded central overheads are, at least in part, reflecting the manner in which councils are organised, which is distinct from the efficiency or otherwise of their operations. Districts also have many more direct dealings with members of the public than do the counties (Wilks-Heeg and Clayton 2006), implying much greater difficulty for districts to allocate central costs to service headings, and also the greater joint use of facilities. For reasons such as these, the use of the CIPFA data in the simple manner employed by Co. Durham has little meaning. Consequently, the 'new model' saving of £6.5 million p.a. should be entirely discounted; on that basis, there would be no need to adjust the transition costs on account of the associated job losses. However the matter is regarded, Co. Durham were claiming substantial savings under the 'new model' on the flimsiest of grounds and without including the associated severance costs in the estimate of transition costs but the DCLG did not raise any query about the 'new model' in their February letter.

*Other cases*
It would be tedious to plough through all of the other instances where unrealistic estimates were made for recurrent savings that were not challenged by the DCLG in February 2007, and we will content ourselves with just two further examples. A striking case is the figure of £2.5 million of annual savings claimed by Somerset on account of home working by members of staff. This had nothing to do with re-structuring, and most of the gain could in any case be made by the county council as the larger employer in the county/district system; the sum should be ignored. Cornwall claimed that they could generate £1 million p.a. of extra revenue managing the aggregate district reserves, a claim that implied obtaining a rate of return 1.2 percentage points higher than the districts received. An increase in the rate of return of that magnitude was not plausible even if the county were to follow a high risk/high return investment strategy.

## *Offsetting costs under-estimated: area governance*

Considerable play was made with proposals for devolved governance within unitary counties, with various versions of area committees, the number of which ranged from 14 in Co. Durham to 27 in Shropshire. Citizens were being offered the prospect of real devolution, so that communities would have a greater say over policy and service delivery. The trouble is that the proposed area governance arrangements were either not costed (Somerset), or, as shown in Table 3.1, the sums proposed were very small, as little as £0.9 million in two cases, or £33,000 p.a. for each of the area committees proposed in Shropshire. These figures were not challenged by the DCLG, who seem to have been content to allow themselves to be persuaded that there would be real Neighbourhood empowerment despite the meagre resources proposed for the purpose.

The nature of the problem was particularly clear in Cornwall. Responding to criticisms of their business case, the county said:

> *If the unitary proposal is accepted, the new council would set the overall operational budgets for services and their capital programmes. Depending on the service, the devolution of this budget may be considered. This will not represent an additional draw on the authority's budget, merely a change of the geographical scale at which decisions on priorities are taken. If this devolution takes place, it will occur within an agreed framework for measuring and monitoring both expenditure and performance to agreed targets.* (Cornwall CC 2007a, Appendix 1, para. 10.)

This passage sets out as clearly as is possible that there was no certainty there would be any real devolution, and that if there were to be devolution it would be so constrained that it would offer little real 'empowerment'. A few deckchairs could be re-arranged locally, but the course of the Titanic would be controlled from the centre. The further point to note is the following. If there were to be genuine devolution of budgets, then there would automatically be increased costs because there would have to be the local resources to determine the local priorities and control the spending. It is not true that there would be no additional 'draw on the authority's budget'.

The offers of devolved area governance in county unitary authorities had little substance. Were there to be genuine local empowerment, then the costs would be substantially greater than was projected. The implication is clear, that genuine Neighbourhood empowerment would cost considerably more than was proposed. If we consider just the five counties that are proceeding to unitary status, genuine Neighbourhood empowerment would involve offsetting costs that would be several multiples of the £13.5 million noted on page 53, sufficient to reduce the net annual savings to a paltry sum. But the Government showed no sign of being interested in the minimal financial provision proposed.

### Conclusion on the rigour of the DCLG examination

Enough has been said to show beyond any reasonable doubt that the February/March examination of the financial cases by the DCLG and the subsequent enquiries were a long way from being thorough. Indeed, one is forced to conclude that examination by the DCLG was superficial and very largely pointless. That this was the view of the local authorities themselves during the consultation period has been indicated by what happened with the proposals that have been examined above and is confirmed by one final example.

In the week beginning 14 May 2007, there was a meeting of the county and district treasurers in Cornwall. At that meeting, the county treasurer privately acknowledged that they were budgeting about £30 million for transition costs (Paul Hamill, Pers. comm, 17 May 2007). That figure was about 50% higher than the figure given in the county's bid document, and remarkably close to, though somewhat higher than, the figure of £27.8 million estimated by Chisholm in a critique of the county's case completed on 10 May. Clearly, the county thought that they could get away with a significant under-estimation of transition costs, and in the event they were proved right.

### Further difficulties with the financial data

Two matters have been touched upon above that now deserve explicit examination: the distinction between gross and net costs and savings; and the range of items to be included in the assessments. Linked to these two matters is a third, the very considerable variation in both the absolute size of the estimated costs and savings, and the relationship between the two in particular cases.

### *Gross and net figures*

Table 4.1 sets out the headline figures for transition costs and recurrent savings in the majority of the bid documents submitted to the DCLG in January 2007. In all the cases shown, the gross cost of transition would be identical to the net cost, because there would be no income arising from the transition process; the transition costs can be likened to a capital investment, designed to yield a long term benefit. However, the majority of the headline figures for annual savings were also presented as gross, even if in the body of the relevant documents certain extra ongoing costs were identified, such as the costs of area governance. The headline figures for annual savings for all bids ought to have been presented net of any offsetting additional costs. This simple fact, revealed by Table 4.1, confirms the unreliability of the costing data.

A minority of bids presented headline figures giving the recurrent savings net of at least some additional recurrent costs - the two separate Cheshire bids, Northumberland and Somerset. For the moment, it is immaterial whether the netting out had been done completely; the critical fact is that there was a division of opinion among the local authorities submitting bids regarding the manner in which the headline figures should be presented. Local authorities had been asked to prepare a 'business case' to support proposals, and no business case worthy of the name would use gross savings instead of net savings for the headline figures. The use of gross savings should not have been permitted because assessments on that basis gave a false impression of what was involved.

At page 54, we noted that the £75 million p.a. that the Government claimed would be saved by creating five unitary counties should be reduced by about £20 million on account of the self-assessed sums allocated for area governance and service re-investment, and the omission of pay equalisation provisions. We have seen that the area governance provisions were so small that there could be no realistic expectation of achieving the Government's declared aims of Neighbourhood empowerment, and that several multiples of the aggregate figure of £13.5 million would be needed. We have also discussed some examples of exaggerated estimates for recurrent savings, including savings on district services in Cornwall and Co. Durham to a total of £12.5 million, and the unrealistic expectation of Cornwall CC that it could obtain £1.0 million p.a. extra investment income – the total coming to £13.5 million. This figure is not an exhaustive tally of the exaggerations but represents the nature and the scale of the problems contained in the estimates, enough to show that implausible claims were made.

Initially, we deducted about £20 million from the headline figure Mr Healey gave for the savings that would occur with the creation of five unitary counties. However, the figure of £20 million contained unrealistically low estimates for area governance, the cost of which would be some multiple of £13.5 million if Neighbourhood empowerment were to be genuine. With that in mind, and the £13.5 million of identified exaggerated savings, it is clear that at least another £30 million ought to be deducted from the gross savings Mr Healey identified. On this basis, Parliament ought to have been told that the five county unitary authorities might achieve 'over £25 million' net savings, one third of the figure given.

The truly worrying thing is that the DCLG did not insist that estimates of recurrent savings should be net, and was prepared to accept gross figures, which were presented to Parliament in justification of structural change. Worse still, Members of Parliament did not protest and insist that they be given proper information. For all the rhetoric that emanates from the Government about 'value for money', etc., this was a fundamental and inexcusable failure in the management of public monies.

### Shropshire

In the draft submission circulated by Shropshire CC in November 2006, the headline figure for transition costs was presented as about £3 million. This figure was a net figure, calculated as follows (Shropshire CC, 2006, para. 225). The county council estimated gross transition costs at £5.2 million but offset £2.2 million by a transfer from the calculation of the way in which Council Tax would be equalised across the county area. Such a transfer would have nothing to do with income generated as a direct consequence of change (e.g., potential release of premises). How the financial implications of Council Tax equalisation would be handled was a matter to be considered in respect of current revenue and hence annual savings. It was not admissible to transfer sums from the equalisation calculations, to reduce the apparent cost of change.

By the time the formal submission was made in January 2007, the county had amended the transition cost to £5 million gross, a change that may have been occasioned by the appearance on 10 January of Chisholm's critique of the bid document. It seems reasonable to conclude that in the autumn of 2006 the county had thought they could get away with a fundamentally wrong and misleading way of presenting transition costs and that they might well have persisted had they not been challenged.

### Confusion regarding the items to be costed

That there were uncertainty and confusion about the items to be included in the financial case to back a unitary bid cannot be doubted, but why? The answer is that the DCLG did not set out a checklist of the headings to be considered in assessing the financial implications of reorganisation and, indeed, changed the rules part way through the process.

### The DCLG changed the rules

When bids were submitted in January 2007, it was reasonable to suppose that, if there were to be a unitary county or two unitary authorities for a county area, there would be a reduction in grant income for the 'cost of being in business', the annual sum being £0.325 million for each local authority irrespective of its size. For example, if a county had six districts and became a unitary authority, then £1.950 million p.a. of grant income would be foregone. Some bids incorporated this reduction, but others assumed that the grants would continue. In the event, the DCLG announced part through the consultation period that the grants would be continued as part of the block grant, at least for a few years.

The other change related to the idea of shadow authorities. Considerable play was made by the DCLG that unitary councils would be 'new', and many of the bids for unitary counties included estimates for the cost of electing and then running shadow councils, but not all the bids made this provision. Come the circulation of draft Orders in the autumn of 2007 to implement proposed unitary councils, it became clear that some counties would be treated as continuing authorities, obviating the need for shadow councils. The 5 December announcement that five unitary counties would be created gave 1 April 2009 as the vesting day for all of them, with elections to be held in May 2008 in Co. Durham and Northumberland, and May 2009 in Cornwall, Shropshire and Wiltshire. Despite the commitment to shadow authorities announced in October 2006 (Table 2.1), the policy has not been applied consistently. Some of the counties had included the cost of a shadow authority in their estimation of transition costs, others had not.

### No checklist of items to be considered

By this point in the discussion, the reader will be well aware that the items included in the assessment of costs and savings varied considerably from one proposal to another, and in a manner that seems to have been arbitrary. That this was indeed the case is shown by Table 4.3 for transition costs and Table 4.4 for recurrent savings. The reason for this variation lies in the absence of a standard checklist, a fundamental initial failure from which the LGR did not recover. The costings prepared in support of proposals were not comparing like with like.

## Table 4.4
### Recurrent costs
### Items omitted from bidders' headline estimates

Devolved governance      Somerset

Pay harmonisation      Cheshire (×2), Cornwall[1], Co. Durham, Exeter, Northumberland[2], North Yorkshire, Shropshire, Wiltshire

1. Responding to the DCLG's February 2007 enquiries, Cornwall CC claimed that pay harmonisation had been taken account of by using county pay rates in building up staffing structures but no details were vouchsafed.

2. Northumberland CC included £2.8 million in their transition costs for the 'year of set up'. However, pay harmonisation is not a transition cost but an on-going cost, and a separate breakdown showed the aggregate as spread over five years, at about £0.55 million p.a.

NB Cheshire CC excluded pay harmonisation from their 'bottom up' modelling but included £1 million p.a. in their 'top down' version. Somerset CC estimated a figure of £0.5 million.

It is generally recognised that county councils are apt to pay more for comparable jobs than do district councils. On transferring from one employer to another, employees enjoy salary protection for a limited time under TUPE, and Single Status Agreements are supposed to be revenue neutral. In practice, it is almost inevitable that there would be some upward wage drift, and a figure of £0.5 to £1.0 million for a county unitary seems probable.

---

*Pay harmonisation*

Three of the proposals submitted included a figure for pay harmonisation, at £0.5 million p.a. in one version of the proposal by Cheshire CC and in the case of Northumberland, and £1 million in Somerset. Other proposals omitted any costing, despite the fact that in February 2007 the DCLG raised the matter with a number of councils.

The issue is straightforward in principle but complex in reality. When a unitary council is created, it will be necessary to amalgamate two or more separate workforces into one organisation. When this happens, the Transfer of Undertaking Protection of Employment (TUPE) regulations ensure that there will be protection for individuals against an impoverishment of their terms and conditions for about one year. After that, the new employer will need to negotiate new terms with the inherited employees, or recruit new staff. In addition, there are Single Status Agreements, based on job evaluation, which, in theory, should have no net impact on salary costs because the evaluation is based on relative worth. It appears that the DCLG was willing to accept claims that the over-all effect of these provisions would ensure no upward drift of employment costs. The structural problem with that position is that, in general, county councils have higher pay scales than districts and employ substantially more staff. This provides a one-way ratchet: impossible to amalgamate staff and achieve a net reduction in average employment costs; very difficult to avoid some upward drift.

For these reasons, a conservative estimate is that there would be extra employment costs of £0.5 million p.a. in creating a unitary county, or £2.5 million for five counties, to be set against recurrent savings. The figure comes out at £2.5 million despite the fact that Northumberland estimated £0.5 million, because this county incorrectly treated pay harmonisation as a transition cost and therefore did not deduct the cost from the gross savings claimed.

**The relationships between transition costs and recurrent savings**
Table 4.1 shows that the relationships between estimated transition costs and the expected revenue savings for the various bids provides food for thought. A transition cost of £9.8 million for Shropshire, as estimated in February 2007, may be compared with £21.1 million for a unitary Cheshire; Shropshire's gross saving of £7.8 million was similarly dwarfed, this time by Somerset's figure of £27.2 million. These differences cannot be accounted for by the variation in the size of the county areas, measured by population, area or number of districts. They were largely an artefact of the way the various bids were constructed – the coverage of the estimates and the assumptions employed for the constituent items.

Equally notable is the variation shown in Table 4.1 of the ratio between transition costs and recurrent savings. For seven of the bids, the full annual savings would repay transition costs in about one year, plus or minus, but in four cases the time taken for this repayment to happen would be substantially less, at six months or just a little over, these latter cases being county unitaries in Bedfordshire, Co. Durham and Somerset, and Exeter as unitary city. This pattern, along with the claim that two unitary authorities in Cheshire would yield a higher rate of return than a single unitary, should have alerted the DCLG to the uncertainties there were regarding the estimates of costs and savings, and should have prompted investigation.

It will be recollected that, in July, the DCLG was concerned that dividing up county functions would result in a loss of scale economies in all six of the sub-county proposals, even though the Department was minded to proceed with four of these six cases (Table 2.3), two of which were ultimately successful – a unitary Bedford and two unitary councils in Cheshire. Given the worries about loss of scale economies, it would be reasonable to expect that the annual savings for sub-county unitary authorities would be lower than for unitary counties, and especially if those savings are calculated per resident in the unitary councils. Table 4.1 shows that the self-assessments for Bedford and for two unitaries in Cheshire suffered from no such inhibitions regarding the aggregate sums claimed, with results that are surprising when converted to savings per inhabitant (Table 4.5).

Among the proposals listed in Table 4.5, a unitary Bedford was estimated to give annual savings of almost £48 per person, compared with the lowest unitary county estimates of less than half that sum. The ambitious savings claimed for two unitaries in Cheshire would give savings per person significantly higher than estimated by Cheshire CC, and even the lower figure accepted by the DCLG places the proposal among the counties with the lowest savings claimed. The position of these two sub-county unitary proposals in relation to the ten county unitaries indicates that, for these two proposals, the DCLG suspended its concerns about the loss of scale economies. In the absence of an explanation from the Department, it is difficult to reach any conclusion other than that the Government acted irrationally.

### The use, misuse and abuse of consultants

Several authorities referred to the use of professional consultants to check their financial cases, either as part of the original bid documentation or subsequently during the consultation period. The purpose of these references was to provide credibility for the figures that had been submitted. However, one needs to be cautious in accepting the claims, for the following basic reason. In principle, a consultant could be asked two questions:

1. Are the assumptions reasonable?

2. Given the assumptions, is the arithmetic accurate?

## Table 4.5
Estimates of gross annual savings per head of population
Unitary counties plus two unitaries in Bedfordshire and Cheshire

| | Population June 2006 000 | Annual savings £ million[1] | £/hd of population |
|---|---|---|---|
| North Yorkshire | 579.9 | 14.0 | 21.4 |
| **Cheshire, 2 unitaries** | **679.8** | **16.0** | **23.5** |
| Cornwall | 523.9 | 15.0 | 28.6 |
| Shropshire | 288.8 | 9.0 | 31.2 |
| Cheshire, 1 unitary | 679.8 | 26.8 | 39.4 |
| Wiltshire | 449.7 | 18.0 | 40.0 |
| Co. Durham | 492.1 | 21.0 | 42.7 |
| **Cheshire, 2 unitaries** | **679.8** | **30.1[2]** | **44.3** |
| Cumbria | 494.8 | 22.7 | 45.9 |
| **Bedfordshire, 2 unitaries** | **392.6** | **18.7** | **47.6** |
| Somerset | 520.4 | 27.2 | 52.3 |
| Northumberland | 307.0 | 17.0 | 55.4 |
| Bedfordshire, 1 unitary | 392.6 | 26.6 | 67.8 |

1. Most recent figures shown in Table 4.1 except for the higher figure for two unitary councils in Cheshire.

2. The savings figure as 'validated' by Deloitte, September 2007.

NB The population figures have been taken from CIPFA 2006.

If both questions have been posed and answered, then one knows where one stands and the report may well be good. However, if the first question is omitted, the exercise is called in question. If no answer is given to either question, then time and money would have been wasted, which is exactly what happened in Cornwall.

Cornwall's steadfast support in June for the figures that had been submitted in January has already been noted (p. 57), including the claim that Price Waterhouse Coopers (PWC) had 'verified' the county's financial analysis. Because the PWC document had not been included in the county's documentation, the county solicitor was asked for a copy, which was duly sent to Chisholm on 29 June. The document in question was a letter to the county council, dated 15 January 2007, containing the following relevant text:

> *In reviewing the documentation* [supplied] *we have made no assumptions regarding the achievability of the efficiency savings or the integrity and accuracy of the information contained within the financial spreadsheet. We have not carried out a due diligence exercise on the supporting information. The views expressed in this letter do not form the basis of a formal audit opinion on the figures used in the council's submission … In particular no responsibility is taken or accepted by PriceWaterhouseCoopers LLP and all liability is excluded by PriceWaterhouseCoopers LLP for the accuracy of computations comprised therein and the assumptions upon which such computations are based.*

PWC had not verified Cornwall's figures. The public claim by the county that their figures had been accepted by PWC was untrue and should have been known to be untrue.

PWC were commissioned by a number of bidders, and in Wiltshire's case they did more work than for Cornwall. Their report was included as an appendix to the county's January submission. The company made it clear that their work was a 'preliminary' report about 'potential' costs and savings in Wiltshire, with the qualification about recurrent savings that they represented the 'eventual potential' financial benefit, and the general observation that there was the need to 'further review and refine the figures'. It was proper for PWC to emphasise the preliminary and tentative nature of the financial estimates. However, PWC claimed to have provided 'a combination of analysis, advice, support and challenge' but they failed to draw attention to significant omissions from the list of topics to be costed in assessing annual savings, notably area governance and the cost of pay assimilation (the figure of £0.9 million for area governance was supplied by the county subsequently). PWC reported gross annual savings, not net savings, and this is the manner in which the county presented their case. There were distinct limits to the willingness of PWC to challenge the assumptions being made by the council.

Cheshire CC also used PWC to assist them in evaluating their own unitary county bid, the two unitary proposal and improved two tier working. In the January submission, there was a single paragraph, claiming that PWC had judged the county's estimates in all three cases to be 'reasonable', but no documentation was provided. The following June, the county's document (2007b) listed three PWC papers as 'supplied separately', although it turned out that they could only be obtained as a Freedom of Information request. The 'reasonableness' test for the county's own submission consisted of the following exercise. Using the self-assessments of all ten county unitary bids as at 14 June 2007, the positions of Cheshire in the rankings for several financial criteria were obtained. The rankings were for per caput use of reserves, transition costs and recurrent savings. On the basis of this information, PWC concluded as follows:

> *As can be seen, for all of key financial metrics, Unitary Cheshire is around the median value when benchmarked against all the County Council submissions* (PWC 2007, p. 3).

An equivalent approach had been adopted by PWC in the report included in Wiltshire's January bid document.

This approach to the test of reasonableness makes two fundamental assumptions: that the estimates had been prepared with the same coverage of items; and that the estimation of the items included was robust in all cases. Neither of these assumptions was examined by PWC and, as we have seen, neither assumption stands up to scrutiny. The procedure adopted by PWC was no real test of the figures, being little more than a circular argument.

On behalf of those proposing two unitary councils in Cheshire, Deloitte undertook an 'independent validation' of the figures that had been submitted to the DCLG in June, the document being completed in September 2007. Two features of this 'validation' are worth noting in the present context. With respect to transition costs, Deloitte were willing to accept a zero entry for IT costs on the following grounds:

*Assumed that ICT systems are not split and existing County network and systems will be shared/utilised. New systems required will be met from existing ICT Capital budgets.* (Deloitte 2007, p. 10.)

On the other hand, the consultants supported the figure of £6 million p.a. for IT cost savings, giving the following reasons:

*Establishment of a single ICT support mechanism to support systems within each organisation will enable full utilisation of technology to provide relevant services. Current Capital funding budgeted in baseline at c£7m.* (Deloitte 2007, pp. 31-2.)

Deloitte were willing to 'validate' an annual IT saving of £6 million that related to existing investment programmes and had nothing to do with structural reorganisation. They were also willing to accept that there would be zero transition costs for accommodation and contract novation. Their estimate for staff release costs gave a figure of £68,000 per person, but the comparison made with other authorities' bids used a figure of about £20,000. They also failed to point out that an annual saving of £44.3 per resident was implausible in the context of the county bids shown in Table 4.5 and the improbability of maintaining scale economies despite dividing the county into two.

At this juncture, the reader may reasonably observe that, if there were problems with the work undertaken by professional accountancy firms employed by those submitting bids, then was this weakness not also true of the work we undertook on behalf of objectors, jointly in Cheshire, and by Chisholm elsewhere? We were asked to examine bids that had been submitted, to evaluate their strengths and weaknesses, and to do so on the basis of evidence so far as was possible. We do not claim to be infallible, but we do claim to have produced argued and evidenced documents in which a clear distinction was drawn between what could be accepted and that which was questionable. To our knowledge, three of the bidding authorities chose to issue rebuttal documents, documents that had the following characteristics in common in varying degree – dismissal, misrepresentation and abuse.

The proponents of two unitary councils in Cheshire dismissed Chisholm's work with just these words:

> *Professor Chisholm has been engaged by authorities seeking the continuation of two tier working in Cheshire and across other areas in the country* (Cheshire JDC 2007a, p. 3).

The clear implication was that anyone engaged by those seeking to maintain a two tier structure must necessarily produce a worthless document. No reasoned argument was offered to show what mistakes had been made. Cheshire CC gave credit that Chisholm 'sought to be objective' but then misrepresented the 'two-way correspondence', omitting to mention a telephone discussion in which he ended by saying that it would be necessary to agree to differ. Most of the specific points raised by the county were stated in general terms without any detail as to how they impacted on the cost and saving estimates (Cheshire CC 2007a). As for Cornwall, the county issued a rebuttal (Cornwall CC 2007a) containing numerous deliberate misrepresentations of the critical comments; there was also a press release about a leaflet issued by districts, which leaflet set out comments from the county's bid and relevant ones from Chisholm's critique. The language used by the county about that critique included the following: superficial, misinformation, myths, totally misrepresents the facts, almost entirely without merit. Yet the county treasurer had estimated a transition cost close to, but somewhat above, the figure derived by Chisholm (see p. 70).

Clearly, the use of external financial consultants hired by interested parties cannot be relied upon to provide quality assurance of the financial documentation. At least in some cases, and despite claims by the bidding authority, professional consultants did not audit or verify the financial data contained in bid documents. Instead, they provided documents equivalent to the inadequate 'comfort letters' written for Northern Rock before its financial crisis in the autumn of 2007. The Northern Rock letters were inadequate because the authors were not asked to consider liquidity problems, the very issue that caused the collapse. The parallel with the LGR was the limited remit to which consultants were asked to work.

## DCLG summary of stakeholder responses

It was in November 2007 that the DCLG issued its summary of the responses it had received during the formal consultation period, 27 March to 22 June 2007. This document included some general tabulations and also separate brief accounts of the responses received for each of the sixteen proposals. These accounts provide comments on the responses of local authorities to the respective financial cases put forward in support of unitary bids. The nature of these financial observations is conveyed by the selection reported in Table 4.6. In all these cases, nothing further was said, so that the information about the DCLG's summaries contained in the table is complete for the particular cases.

Compare the terms reported in Table 4.6 with the selection of detailed issues discussed earlier in this chapter. All of those details, and many more besides, were included in the documentation submitted by local authorities during the consultation period. There is no sense that the precise and detailed criticisms have been understood by the DCLG, examined and either found to be wanting or were accepted. Indeed, we

---

**Table 4.6**

The DCLG's financial comments on individual proposals
November 2007

| | |
|---|---|
| Cornwall | Districts were concerned about 'what they saw as inaccuracies in the business case.' |
| Co. Durham | 'All the district councils in County Durham were opposed to the unitary proposal, questioning in particular the robustness of the proposal's financial case.' |
| Exeter | 'Devon County Council questioned the business case …' |
| Shropshire | Districts were concerned 'that the cost of change had increased compared to the original predictions.' |
| Somerset | 'Reasons for opposition included the cost of transition and the realism of projected savings, which, it was argued, could be achieved without a unitary council.' |
| Wiltshire | 'District councils expressed concerns about the proposal, particularly in relation to the affordability [criterion] … and submitted their own prospectus for improved two-tier working.' |

NB The DCLG did not always comment on the financial cases, even at the level shown above.

Source: DCLG 2007a.

know that, for all practical purposes, all the financial queries and criticisms of the five successful county bids were rejected by the DCLG, but no explanation has been vouchsafed. Beyond any reasonable doubt, the Secretary of State's judgement, reported to Parliament on 5 December 2007, that the self-assessed estimates for the five successful counties 'will' yield annual savings in excess £75 million, cannot be accepted as genuinely based on all the evidence submitted.

### The Government refused to publish the independent financial assessments it commissioned

During the House of Commons debate on the Government's Order to implement the creation of two unitary councils in Cheshire, the late Mrs Gwyneth Dunwoody, one of the local Members, made the following observation:

> *The savings have changed, the administration costs have changed and it is very clear that the information given to the Government was not strong enough to support their view - otherwise, they would have been quite prepared to support the request made under the Freedom of Information Act for a copy of the assessment and would not have needed to refuse it. If the report vindicates the decision further to change the financial envelope, why does the Department wish to conceal it? There must be a reason.* (Hansard 26 February 2008, col. 1049.)

Mr John Healey, the Minister for Local Government, had this to say in response:

> *I should say that we have not disclosed the detail of the independent financial assessment; that was conducted as advice to Ministers and was therefore covered by section 35 as an exemption from freedom of information requirements. However, I have made clear the principal conclusions of the assessment.* (Hansard, 26 February 2008, col. 1062.)

A debate in the Grand Committee of the House of Lords on 21 February had revealed that the Government had employed consultants to examine the financial cases for the new unitary structures then the subject of Orders for implementation (*Hansard* 21 February, col. GC 26). With that knowledge, and unaware of Mr Healey's statement, Chisholm wrote to the DCLG on 26 February seeking access to the consultants' reports for the five county unitaries and the two unitary proposal for Cheshire, doing so as an FOI request. No other information was sought. Once it was known that Members of Parliament had been denied access to the financial consultant's report for Cheshire, the expectation was that Chisholm's request would be politely but firmly rejected. Consequently, it was surprising to receive a letter, dated 1 April 2008, part of which read:

*We confirm that we do hold information falling within the terms of your request. However, some of the information you requested falls within qualified exemptions in the Freedom of Information Act 2000. In relation to this information we are still considering whether the public interest in disclosure is outweighed by the public interest in non-disclosure.*

At the very minimum, it is clear that the left hand of the DCLG does not know what the right hand is doing, a matter of considerable public interest. The book went to press before the substantive answer had been received.

Until or unless the consultants' reports are made public, it is impossible to know the terms of reference given to those who conducted the financial reviews, and how thorough they may have been in checking the assumptions and the arithmetic contained in the documents submitted by those proposing unitary structures. Nor can one tell whether criticisms discussed in this chapter were addressed. Which is all a polite way of wondering whether the Government's consultants were any more reliable than some of those used in support of bids, and whether Mr Healey was any more open about the 'principal conclusions' of the financial advice than the DCLG had been in summarising the March-June consultation responses.

The non-disclosure stance taken by the Government on this matter is all the more troubling when we recall the following. In October 2006, the invitation issued by the DCLG said that, in the first stage of the process after proposals had been received in January 2007, the Department would proceed by using the following assumption:

*Where information is not available to the Government, or otherwise, the Government may when considering a proposal make such assumptions and estimates as it sees fit* (DCLG 2006b, para. 5.6).

Had the Department said that it would make assumptions and estimates that it deemed to be reasonable, the whole process would have been conducted in the knowledge that there could be challenges if there were grounds for believing that it had acted unreasonably. Instead, a form or words was chosen giving the Department licence to do what it liked, irrespective of evidence and reasonableness.

## Conclusion

For all practical purposes, the figure of £75 million reported to Parliament as the annual savings from creating five unitary councils represents gross savings, from which there need to be deductions. The initial deduction identified was about £20 million, for the self-assessed area governance costs and service re-investment costs, plus pay harmonisation costs. We have seen that the area governance costs estimated in the bids were so small that they could not provide for the Neighbourhood empowerment desired by the Government. We have also seen that some of the individual claims for savings were so questionable that they should have been disallowed in what were supposed to be 'business plans' to support unitary proposals, the three illustrative cases identified accounting for £13.5 million in Cornwall and Co. Durham alone. This last figure demonstrates the doubts that surround many of the estimated savings, and must not be treated as an exhaustive analysis. Taken together, these admittedly incomplete figures imply further deductions of at least £30 million, which would reduce the 'over £75 million' saving reported by Mr Healey to a net figure 'over £25 million' p.a., not all of which would become available from vesting day, there being a time-lapse for savings to build up.

On the other side of the ledger, it is also clear beyond any reasonable doubt that transition costs have been under-estimated, by the exclusion of items such as IT costs, and by assessments that seriously under-state the scale of expenditure needed. At the beginning of this chapter, we noted that the aggregate transition costs estimated by the five counties amounted to £77 million. We have also noted that the county treasurer for Cornwall was privately willing to admit to transition costs 50% greater than was publicly acknowledged in the county's bid. Chisholm reviewed four of the five successful county bids, Cornwall included. In aggregate for these counties, his estimate for transition costs exceeded the amount estimated in the bids by 55%, close to the excess acknowledged by Cornwall's treasurer. This indicates that the £77 million transition cost for the five counties should be increased by about 50%, making a figure of about £116 million the realistic figure to consider for the total transition cost.

These orders of magnitude for transition costs and recurrent savings are based on the incomplete evidence adduced in this book. They demonstrate that savings probably would not repay the costs of change within five years. That being the case, it was unlikely that the Affordability criterion would be met for the five counties collectively, and that calls in question their performance on Value for money.

In addition, it is difficult to reconcile the anxieties that the DCLG had in July about the loss of scale economies if counties were divided with the decisions to create two unitary councils in both Bedfordshire and Cheshire. The DCLG did not explain why the July concerns were set aside.

The financial data accepted by the DCLG were unreliable. It is hard to avoid the conclusion that the Secretary of State, relying on deficient information, acted irrationally in the decision process, and that Parliament was misled.

# 5

# Opinions of stakeholders and the public

Some aspects of the consultation process and the Department's evaluation thereof have been alluded to in previous chapters, most notably references to the 'climate' in which public opinion polls were conducted (Chapter 3) and the exiguous nature of the assessments of the financial cases (Chapter 4). This chapter examines these matters in more detail in the light of the document issued by the DCLG in November 2007, their Summary of Responses (DCLG 2007a). We already know from Chapter 4 that the November document provided very little real information on financial matters and therefore failed to explain the way in which the Department had handled that material in the unitary proposals. We also know that serious information could not have been available about the reactions of stakeholders, partners and the public at the time proposals were submitted in January 2007, making it particularly important to understand how matters stood with regard to revealed attitudes at the end of the consultation period in June. Therefore, the central purpose of this chapter is to review the November document in the light of available information, to see whether the DCLG summarised the responses of stakeholders and the public adequately.

### The DCLG handled the consultation
From the outset, it was made clear that the Department would handle the whole consultation and decision process up to the laying of Orders before Parliament. Consequently, all proposals were submitted to the Department, as also all representations made thereon. The bald statistics are set out in Table 5.1, summarising the volume of responses received

by the DCLG in the period 27 March to 22 June from various interests identified. In addition, there are certain features of the consultation process that need to be set out clearly to aid our understanding of what went on.

When the Local Government and Public Involvement in Health Bill was published early in the LGR process, it contained Section 4 on the procedure to be followed by the Secretary of State upon receipt of unitary proposals. At 4(2), the Bill provided that all local authorities must be consulted if the proposal were not submitted jointly by all the relevant councils, and that where there was a lack of unanimity among the councils the Secretary of State must also consult 'any other person he believes to have an interest' in the proposal. In the event of unanimity among the local authorities, the Secretary of State may consult any other person he believes to have an interest. It was reasonable to assume that the terms of the Bill provided the framework within which the consultation would be conducted.

However, when the legislation reached the statute book, the whole of Section 4 had been removed. More to the point, Ministers decided that they would not themselves actively consult members of the public, even though it is difficult to see how they could believe that citizens did not 'have an interest' in re-organisation proposals for their area.

### The DCLG's web-page
In accordance with the provision contained in Section 4(2) of the Bill, the DCLG did consult all the local authorities affected by the unitary proposals. Although the Department's web-page provided links to the web-pages of authorities proposing structural reorganisation, there were no links to web-pages that had material hostile to unitary bids, most notably those of local authorities. At the September 2007 hearing of the judicial review brought by Shrewsbury and Congleton, it was argued on behalf of the DCLG that it had no statutory duty to provide links to any antagonistic web-pages, even if the number were limited to just the local authorities affected by a proposal. Although Mr Justice Underhill felt obliged to accept this argument as a correct statement of the law, during the course of the hearing he was acerbic about the DCLG's failure to ensure a level playing field for the consultation (see Chapter 6). The Department's decision had the effect of providing unequal ease of access to material for and against proposals, biasing the process in favour of unitary outcomes

## Table 5.1
## Summary of the consultation responses directly received by the DCLG
## Number of responses by eight categories of respondent

|  | 1 | 2 | 3 | 4 | 5 | 6 | 7 | 8 |
|---|---|---|---|---|---|---|---|---|
| Bedfordshire | 7 | 15 | 18 | 6 | 7 | 41 | 94 | 30,300 |
| Cheshire | 27 | 64 | 67 | 35 | 33 | 680 | 906 | 200 |
| Cornwall | 15 | 59 | 25 | 11 | 19 | 422 | 551 | 1,750 |
| Cumbria | 11 | 40 | 25 | 21 | 13 | 310 | 420 | 1,700 |
| Co . Durham | 10 | 21 | 39 | 24 | 21 | 149 | 264 | 325 |
| Exeter | 21 | 84 | 51 | 14 | 20 | 352 | 542 | 180 |
| Ipswich | 10 | 80 | 40 | 7 | 18 | 288 | 443 | 125 |
| North Yorkshire | 15 | 78 | 25 | 25 | 50 | 706 | 899 | 130 |
| Northumberland | 9 | 26 | 22 | 24 | 16 | 93 | 190 | 3,400 |
| Norwich | 15 | 64 | 28 | 15 | 15 | 1,496 | 1,633 | 2,000 |
| Shropshire | 16 | 18 | 24 | 15 | 21 | 138 | 232 | 0 |
| Somerset | 7 | 13 | 14 | 8 | 12 | 57 | 111 | 1,700 |
| Wiltshire | 14 | 73 | 16 | 18 | 16 | 201 | 338 | 6,500 |
| Total | 177 | 635 | 394 | 223 | 261 | 4,933 | 6,623 | 48,310 |

Responses from:

1.   Local government.
2.   Town and parish councils.
3.   Public sector.
4.   Business sector.
5.   Voluntary and community sector.
6.   Public responses.
7.   Total, excluding campaign responses.
8.   Campaign responses received.

NB  The figures for polls and referenda, and information regarding other stakeholder attitudes, reported by local authorities to DCLG, are excluded.

Source: DCLG 2007a

in some degree, although probably not by very much. Perhaps the most significant aspect of this detail is what it reveals about the attitude of the DCLG to consultation, the sense that consultation is fine so long as you can be sure to get the 'right' answer.

### What voice for members of the public?

When the DCLG issued its invitation to local authorities to submit unitary bids, it was stated that the government would 'consult widely' about the proposals to be taken forward in March 2007 (DCLG 2006b, para. 5.10). This consultation would be with partners and stakeholders in the affected areas. Earlier in the same document, the criterion was set out that proposals must have a broad cross section of support from 'key partners, stakeholders and service users/citizens' (para. 3.5). During the September judicial review hearing, the judge asked the Secretary of State's legal representative whether 'service users' included citizens and received confirmation that this was so. However, the overall impression conveyed by the wording of the invitation document and the discussion in court was that the Government was not willing to accord much significance to the views of the electorate, and this impression was confirmed by the way in which the consultation was handled. The Department wrote to partners and stakeholders in each review area, asking for their comments on proposals, but took no active steps to elicit the reactions of the public in affected areas. Citizens were 'consulted' directly by the Government only in the sense that letters sent by individuals to the Department were 'taken into account' along with all the other submissions.

### How comprehensive was the DCLG's evaluation?

Chapter 4 has touched upon the lack of financial detail in the DCLG's November evaluation, and this deficiency applied all the way through the document. At the most general level, although responses from local authorities were reported, the substance of the information contained in those responses was not identified and incorporated with the summary of material sent direct to the Department. As a result, there was no attempt to summarise all of the material received, that which went to the Department directly and that which was included in submissions from local authorities. The unbalanced nature of the account has already been demonstrated with respect to financial matters and the same defect applied to everything else, as may most easily be seen in the consideration of the 'broad cross section of support'.

It is useful to start with case studies of Cheshire and Co. Durham. Cheshire, it will be recalled, was a county where two competing unitary proposals went forward for consultation, whereas in Co. Durham there was just the unitary county to be considered. In both cases, public opinion polls were discounted in the July letters, on the basis of the 'climate' in which they were undertaken. Curiously, the November document does not refer to the 'climate' in either county, or, indeed, in any of the other cases where the matter was mentioned in July.

## Cheshire

### *Over-all picture*

Table 5.2 reproduces the figures for Cheshire contained in the DCLG's November 2007 summary of responses that had been received up to 22 June. The remainder of the table records an analysis of the responses held on 25 January 2008, undertaken by Jan Griffiths and Robin Levett. Because some additional responses had been received after 22 June, there are small differences in the totals, but the magnitudes are too small to have a material impact on the aggregates identified. Consequently, the patterns of preferences revealed in January will accord very closely with the patterns as they were in June 2007. Note that the local authority responses have not been included in the January 2008 analysis.

Nobody reading the DCLG's November document would have any inkling that only 5.2% of respondents favoured the option of two unitary councils in Cheshire. Even if members of the public are excluded from the tally, the two-unitary proposal was favoured by no more than 7.6% of the respondents. Nor would anyone realise that the two-unitary option came a poor third, after those who favoured a unitary county and the idea of improved two tier arrangements.

For ease of reference, Table 5.2 reproduces excerpts from the November document for three groups of respondents, which excerpts can be compared with the raw data. The words chosen by the Department did not convey explicit untruths, but were highly misleading. In addition to the failure to record the limited support for two unitary councils, note that 196 responses, or 28%, supported continuation of two tiers. As for the schools, it was not true to say that all the respondent schools supported a unitary county: four of the seventeen did not take that position; and, as is shown below, the Cheshire Association of Secondary Headteachers would have opted for the continuation of two tiers if they had believed that to be an option. It is difficult to believe that the misleading nature of the summaries was accidental.

The Government was consulting on two proposals for unitary structures and, viewed dispassionately, the issues should have been posed in the following terms. First, should the two-tier structure be scrapped and replaced with a unitary structure? Second, if so, which of the two options should be preferred? It is clear that the county council itself perceived the issue in these terms, if only because they asked PWC to review the option of an improved two tier arrangement as an alternative to structural change. The resulting document was cited in the county's June submission to the DCLG (Cheshire CC 2007b). In any case, continuation of the two tier arrangements was manifestly possible in principle for no other reason than the rejection in July of some county unitary bids (e.g., Cumbria) and the fact that structural change was not going to happen in county areas where no bid had been received or had gone forward for consultation in March. Despite these considerations, the Department sought to convey the idea that, in Cheshire, the continuation of two tier arrangements was not an option, a position that was at least consistent with the Government's view as stated to Parliament when debating the Order to create two authorities in Cheshire:

> *Our starting point is that the general case for unitary local government is strong (Hansard 26* February 2008, col. 1043).

### Public opinion

Public opinion was tested in a variety of ways by two of the districts and also by the county. On behalf of Congleton and Crewe & Nantwich, IpsosMORI organised a poll of 1,998 residents throughout Cheshire, this poll being conducted by telephone. Just over half of the respondents (52%) preferred an improved two tier arrangement; 23% wanted two unitary councils; and 16% desired to have a single unitary authority. For Crewe & Nantwich, Electoral Reform Services conducted a postal ballot within the borough of the 88,000 registered electors. The ballot paper and supporting documentation were approved by ERS. With a response rate of 34%, 25,022 individuals indicated their desire for improved two tier arrangements, this being 85% of the valid votes. Support for one or other of the unitary options amounted to only 15%. Both organisations have well established and deserved reputations for conducting their enquiries in as impartial a manner as is possible.

## Table 5.2
### Cheshire: number of consultation responses received by the DCLG
### Excludes responses from local authorities

| | Nov. 2007[1] | Analysed January 2008[2] | | | | |
|---|---|---|---|---|---|---|
| | | Total | 2×U | 1×U | Impr.[d] 2-tier. | Undecided/ don't know or care |
| Parish/town councils | 64 | 66 | 5 | 15 | 33 | 13 |
| Public sector | 67 | 63 | 5 | 48 | 7 | 3 |
| Business sector | 35 | 34 | 3 | 26 | 2 | 3 |
| Voluntary/community sector | 33 | 35 | 2 | 24 | 1 | 8 |
| Public responses | 680 | 688 | 31 | 441 | 196 | 20 |
| Total | 879 | 886 | 46 | 554 | 239 | 47 |
| *Individual schools*[3] | - | *18* | *1* | *14* | *3* | *0* |

1.  Figures reported in DCLG (2007a), covering the period 27 March to 22 June 2007. No figures given for individual schools.

2.  The files were examined by Jan Griffiths and Robin Levett on 25 January 2008.

3.  The school figures are a sub-set of the public sector responses.

**Excerpts from the DCLG November text:**
**Parish and town councils.** *About a quarter of responses received from town and parish councils expressed a preference for the single unitary option … A small number favoured the two unitary option, whilst many considered that improved two-tier working should have been an option.*

**Public sector.** *The majority of responses from the public sector organisations expressed support for one of the* [unitary] *proposals, although a small minority were eager to strengthen the existing two-tier system …*
*All schools that submitted evidence expressed a preference for the Cheshire county option.*

**Members of the public.** *Although some members of the public wrote to express support for the two unitary proposal, the great majority of representations received from members of the public expressed support for the County's proposal. Many felt that having a single council for Cheshire would raise the standard of service provision for all county residents. Others expressed their concern at a perceived lack of accountability within district councils, an issue they felt would be ameliorated by a single authority. Others considered that Cheshire County's proposals would make local government in Cheshire more consistent with other parts of the country.*

The county council used several means for measuring public opinion – face-to-face interviews by BMG Research, a feedback questionnaire on the county's website, telephone interviews and focus groups. The only one of these about which full details have been made public by the county is the BMG study, based on 1,001 interviews. The county council stated that this survey showed 43% of respondents choosing a unitary county and 36% as wanting two unitary councils (Cheshire CC 2007b, p. 23). However, these answers were in response to a question that assumed that continuation of the status quo was not an option, so that members of the public were asked to choose between a single unitary council or two unitaries for the county, or to state that they did not know.

Immediately prior to being asked to choose only between the two unitary options, respondents had been asked to choose from the following possibilities (the percentage results are shown):

1. 'A unitary system which would reduce the number of principal councils down from seven to one or two.' 39%

2. 'The existing two tier arrangement should be kept.' 44%

The remaining respondents either had no preference or did not know. These figures were not mentioned by the county council in their June communication to the DCLG.

The figures of 43% and 36% supporting one and two unitary councils were therefore the balance of opinion among the 39% who believed that a unitary structure of one or two councils would be desirable plus those who, actually preferring two tiers, nevertheless felt obliged to select between the two options for unitary local government. The county presented the BMG findings in a misleading way, and must have been done so knowingly.

The other surveys conducted by the county were not described in detail in their June 2007 document, with the consequence that the results cannot be fully assessed. However, the county acknowledged of the write-in responses to their website questionnaire that: 'It is impossible to say how representative those views are'. Nevertheless, those 236 responses were amalgamated with all the other responses obtained by the county, including 1,200 telephone interviews, to summarise the results of all of the surveys with the following words:

*In summary, the single most popular option was the single unitary. More people voted for this than either 2 unitaries or improved Two Tier. Amongst the people who voted unitary, the significant majority was for a single unitary authority.* (Cheshire CC 2007b, p. 22.)

On the evidence discussed above, and on the county's own admission, this statement had little real meaning. Beyond any reasonable doubt, the county misrepresented the results obtained from the tests of public opinion undertaken on its behalf or that it undertook itself.

The single paragraph reproduced in Table 5.2 from the DCLG's November document provided an inadequate summary of public attitudes and misrepresented the overall situation. It is extraordinary that the Department was apparently unaware that write-in responses are notoriously unreliable, a matter to which we will return. It is difficult to avoid the conclusion that the Department's assessment of public opinion cannot be accepted.

### Parish and town councils

Mr Healey, the Minister for Local Government, chose in Parliament to portray the opinions of this group of councils as follows:

*Not only the three district councils back the two-unitary solution – important businesses also do … and six of the 20 parishes that expressed a view do* (Hansard 26 February 2008, col. 1062).

The DCLG had recorded in November that 64 parish and town councils had written to the Department, and when the returns were examined in January 2008, two more responses had been received. Of the 66 responses then on file, five supported two unitary councils, 15 favoured a single council and 33 wanted the two tiers retained (Table 5.2).

As Table 5.2 shows, the general pattern of parish and town council opinion can be worked out from the account given in the DCLG's November document but the results were presented in a misleading manner. Parliament was also given misleading information, but in this case the information was wrong.

Note the fact, recorded by the Department (DCLG 2007a) that many parish and town councils in Cheshire 'considered that two-tier working should have been an option'. This comment reveals more about what was happening in Cheshire than the Department is likely to have intended, proving that the 'climate' of which the Department complained in July was a climate pre-disposed to the idea that structural change was inevitable. For this reason, there will have been a general bias in all of the consultation and polling because respondents felt forced to choose one of the unitary options even if the continuation of two tier working was offered as a possibility, because that possibility would have seemed unrealistic.

### Schools

According to the DCLG in November, all the schools that responded preferred the single unitary option. In January 2008, there were 18 school responses on file at the Department, of which 14 supported a single council, but there were four expressing other preferences. It may be that these four responses had been received after June 2007, but this seems unlikely. In any case, the DCLG chose to ignore the following information. Mr Andy Robinson, on behalf of the executive committee of the Cheshire Association of Secondary Headteachers, wrote to the Department on 14 June 2007, the first substantive paragraph of this letter reading as follows:

> *Given the considerable amount of change that schools and Local Authorities are already engaged in, there would seem to be considerable merit at present in maintaining the current two-tier structure. However, I understand that maintaining the "status quo" is not an option and therefore having given due consideration to the options being proposed the Executive Committee has decided to support the proposal for a single unitary council.*

Under the misapprehension that the preferred two tier arrangement could not continue, the headteachers felt obliged to decide which of the two unitary options being considered would be better from their point of view. This response cannot be construed to be support for change to a single unitary, only that this choice would be less disadvantageous than having two unitary councils.

### The 'climate' in which attitudes were formed

Two examples have been cited above showing that many parishes and also the secondary headteachers believed that continuation of two tier arrangements was not an option and that therefore they had to choose between the two proposals for unitary structures. The same misapprehension was evident in the website of the Campaign to Protect Rural England – Cheshire. They asked their members to write to the DCLG to express their opinions on a single unitary authority or two unitaries for the county. These two options were briefly stated and viewers were directed to two websites for further information. However, the request to write was preceded by the following text:

> *The two-tier structure in the shire ... will be swept away and replaced with either a single Unitary Council ... or two Unitary Councils ... The Government is consulting on these two options.*

It was technically correct to say that the government was consulting on the two options, but incorrect to present this as a consultation merely on which of these options to choose. Whether the CPRE should be blamed for this mistake is an issue dwarfed in importance by the clear evidence that there was an erroneous impression abroad that structural change was inevitable.

The source of this confusion was the Department. In Cheshire, the DCLG acted in the belief that unitary proposals would only be forthcoming from areas where 'local government restructuring is widely seen as the way forward' (p. 10). The presumption for change was actively fostered by the Department, as is shown by the following clear example. On 12 July 2007, Mr Mike Cooksley wrote to Mr David Marren, an officer at Crewe & Nantwich, about the response that he had sent to the Department on behalf of the organisation Visit Chester and Cheshire, which response implied support for a unitary structure of local government. However, in his July letter he said:

> *As a consultee I felt that it was not within the remit of VCC to comment on any other options that might have been available as the Minister had requested responses specifically relating to the two preferred options. ... I must make clear that, the Minister had not asked for comments on this third option* [improved two tier] *and thus this was not within our remit to comment upon!*

Throughout the consultation period, in meetings with local authority representatives, the DCLG gave the impression that improved two tier arrangements were not an option – there would reorganisation to a unitary structure. It was not until a meeting on 8 November that Mr Paul Rowsell acknowledged the principle that two tiers could continue, however unlikely that might be (Glyn Chambers, Pers. comm. 10 December 2007).

Beyond doubt, the 'climate' in Cheshire in which public opinion surveys were undertaken, and stakeholders responded, had a strong bias towards unitary outcomes. Consequently, it seems highly probable that had there been a more equal playing field, the expressions of opposition to structural change would have been more numerous. By complaining about the 'climate' in Cheshire as a reason for discounting the results of opinion polls and referenda, the DCLG was disingenuous.

### Cheshire County Council

Although the county council formally acknowledged that two tiers could continue, they took their cue from the Government and systematically portrayed the options as a choice solely between the two competing unitary proposals. Before the interviews undertaken by BMG began, BMG, in conjunction with the county, mailed an information leaflet to 3,000 potential interviewees, a leaflet prepared by the county. Although this leaflet included the website address of Crewe & Nantwich BC, which authority objected to both of the two unitary proposals for the county, the leaflet itself posed the choice as being about which proposal should be adopted to replace the existing two tiers:

> *The Government has concluded that changes are needed in the way two-tier areas such as Cheshire are run. The Government says the status quo is not an option in two-tier areas if councils are to achieve efficiencies, savings and improvements in service delivery that communities expect, as well as providing value for money. The Government wants to develop Unitary Authorities.*

There then followed a list of seven reasons why the Government was said to want structural change, including such matters as 'confusion' between the tiers, 'better services' and so on. The tenor of this list was that the status quo, i.e., continuation of the two tiers even if improved, was not on the agenda. The information provided in advance to the BMG respondents by the county was biased, making nonsense of the following claim by the county about the leaflet:

> *This was aimed at achieving informed opinions. The County Council was at pains to ensure that the information sent to respondents in advance was as balanced as possible between the two unitary options.*

Despite the bias in the information provided directly to the BMG respondents, leading them to a choice between two unitary structures, maintenance of the existing two tier arrangements was preferred by 44% of those interviewed, with 39% opting for a unitary structure (either one or two authorities for the county area).

Cheshire county council also sought to mobilise their own staff to write to the DCLG direct, the chief executive writing to all employees and an exhortation being placed in the June issue of the in-house newspaper 'Our Cheshire'. This exhortation was framed in terms that would leave the reader in no doubt but that the choice was between one and two unitary councils for the county, the choice being 'how councils across Cheshire should be re-structured', not whether. With about 16,750 full time employee equivalents, compared with approximately 3,280 for the districts, the write-in by county employees could have resulted in a high proportion of the 680 letters received by the DCLG. Perhaps the most significant feature of write-in responses is revealed by the county's own assessment of the returns they themselves received from the questionnaire they had posted on their website. Of the 236 responses received, they noted that: 'It is impossible to say how representative these views are' (Cheshire CC 2007b, p. 24). That observation has to apply to the write-in responses received by the DCLG, not just in Cheshire but everywhere else as well.

In the context set out above, the document issued by Cheshire CC in June seeking to rebut criticisms by Chisholm and Leach, and the Ipsos-MORI poll conducted for districts, makes curious reading. The county went to considerable lengths to show that all surveys of public opinion are influenced by ignorance on the one hand, and campaigns on the other, whereby evidence of opinions in favour of retaining the two tier structure should not be accepted. At one point, they said:

> *A principal reason for not collaborating with Crewe and Nantwich was that the County Council considered the approach they were taking was one-sided and transparently intended to stir up support for a rejection of the Government's proposals* (Cheshire CC 2007a, p. 11).

Overlooking the fact that the proposals being consulted upon were not the Government's but those making bids to the Government, there was a strong sense of the kettle accusing the pot of being black, which is confirmed by the following observations. Having sought to denigrate surveys undertaken by those opposing unitary options, the county then had the following to say:

> *On the issue of Opinion Polls, Cheshire is wholly confident that its methodology would stand up to any objective professional scrutiny for impartiality and sound-ness of method* (Cheshire CC 2007a, p.15).

That claim was not justified, if for no other reason than that the BMG survey was well below the standard normal for such enquiries regarding the information provided in advance and in the way the interview was structured. Furthermore, however well conducted surveys may have been, the results can be presented in many ways that fail to convey the crucial information, which is exactly what the county did in their June document *Building a Sustainable Future.*

It would be wrong to imply that only Cheshire CC succumbed to the temptation to manipulate surveys and to misrepresent the results. However, the evidence is particularly clear in respect of this county, and in varying degree the same sort of thing was widespread in the areas subject to the LGR.

There are two important conclusions to draw from the Cheshire evidence. First, the November document issued by the DCLG was woefully inadequate as a summary of stakeholder and public opinion in the county areas. Second, it gave a misleading impression about the attitudes of stakeholders and the public.

## Co. Durham

The full statement about public attitudes to a unitary Co. Durham contained in the DCLG November document read as follows:

> *Whilst reference was made to the results of polls conducted by district councils, which showed a majority of those who voted being opposed to the proposal, the responses received from the public during the consultation were fairly evenly split between those expressing concerns and those highlighting the benefits of the pro-posal.*

For this county, unlike Cheshire, the existence of opinion polls was recognised in the November consultation summary but, as set out, it would appear that the direct responses had the same significance as the 'polls'. That was thoroughly misleading.

The direct responses numbered 149, meaning that about 75 individuals supported the unitary proposal and a similar number were opposed. Compare those figures with the 'polls', which were not separate enquiries conducted by the districts but a referendum of the 330,000 registered electors in the county, the results of which were reported for each district and in aggregate for the whole county area. The referendum was conducted by Electoral Reform Services, an independent and reputable body. Valid responses were received from 156,306 electors, a response rate of almost 40%. Of the votes cast, 119,439 were in favour of maintaining the existing two-tier structure, 76% of the valid votes. The significance of the 149 direct responses was minimal to zero by comparison, but that is not the impression conveyed by the DCLG.

There was an equivalent problem with the way that the views of parish and town councils were reported by the DCLG:

*Representations from town and parish councils were mixed.*

As Table 5.1 shows, that assessment was based on 21 responses. Communications from parishes and town councils direct to the districts, and reported by them to the DCLG, numbered 32, of which 27 were against a unitary county. This latter set of figures could also be described as 'mixed', but this description would not be helpful. Comparing the two items of evidence, the majority of responding councils, and perhaps a substantial majority, opposed a unitary county.

The third matter in Co. Durham is the manner in which the Department reported the views of the business sector:

*All of the business sector who responded to the consultation expressed broad support for the County proposal, including regional business representative organisations.*

Taken at face value, this statement means that 24 letters of support for a unitary county were received by the DCLG, but there were others who responded to the consultation by submissions to the districts - 138 businesses, of which 107, or 78%, were against the county's proposal. However accurate the DCLG may have been in reporting the responses it had received direct, the fact that other information was ignored means the November document failed to give a correct overall account.

### Bedford

The proposed unitary Bedford provides a particularly striking example of the selectivity and partiality of the DCLG. As already noted (p. 35), the July letter to Bedford BC drew attention to the support their proposal had received from some 30,000 members of the public, making no reference to the 'climate' in which those responses had been obtained. The November DCLG document correctly noted that 'Bedford Borough ran a campaign', but did not make any comment about the impact on the 'climate' of opinion or consider opinion elsewhere in the county.

Prior to submitting their single unitary proposal in January 2007, the county council commissioned IpsosMORI to undertake a survey of 1,000 residents across the county. In response to the first 'cold' question, 49% of respondents backed a single unitary authority, with the proportion rising to 60% at the second time of asking, following the provision of information about the competing proposals. This survey was ignored by the DCLG in the July letters and in the November summary of responses. During the March-June consultation period, Bedfordshire CC did not attempt to elicit information about the level of public support because the DCLG had made it clear to the county that the consultation was with stakeholders and partners, and that therefore public opinion was irrelevant. However, given the terms of the July decision letters and the subsequent invitation for revised unitary proposals for Central Bedfordshire, the county council ran its own petition, obtaining support from more than 30,000 individuals.

With this additional information available, Baroness Andrews, for the Government, had a difficult task in Parliament explaining the balance of opinion in the county between two unitary councils and one:

> *Those divided loyalties were reflected in local polls, and a poll conducted by the county council showed that 46 per cent of those polled preferred the single-unitary proposal. Bedford Borough, however, submitted a petition with over 30,000 signatures in support of its proposal. The county council submitted a petition with 30,000 signatures as part of its 'save our services' campaign. It was very evenly divided, as was stakeholder opinion ... it is fair to say that a majority of representations received from the public sector stakeholders expressed a preference for the county's single-unitary proposal.* (Hansard 25 March 2008, col. GC 103.)

Ignoring factual details, the most significant features of this statement are as follows. First, the Government was obliged to admit that public opinion was divided. Second, an attempt was made to portray attitudes among stakeholders as being equally divided. In fact, the July letter to the county said of the proposed single unitary:

*The Secretary of State acknowledges that most stakeholders who responded from the public, private and third sector support this proposal.*

Elsewhere, public opinion was ignored if it conflicted with the views of stakeholders and partners, but in Bedfordshire the DCLG went out of its way to claim public support to over-ride them.

### Other cases

Some other cases confirm that the DCLG's summary of responses cannot be accepted as an accurate representation of stakeholder and public attitudes. Shrewsbury and Atcham BC in Shropshire commissioned a poll, and the full returns were conveyed to the Department but were sent back – not once, but twice. In other words, the raw evidence was refused. Details of this poll were included in the district's submission, as was the case for other districts in the county. The DCLG summarised this material in the following terms:

*Whilst reference was made to polls undertaken by certain district councils in which a majority of those who voted opposed the unitary proposal, the majority of consultation responses received supported the proposal, with around one third opposing.*

This statement was ambiguous, since it did not specify whether the responses received were from members of the public only, or the total number of direct responses. If the former, the total number was 138 respondents; if the latter, 232. In either case, in the light of the foregoing discussion about Cheshire and Co. Durham, the Department's summary was not a true reflection of local opinion.

Finally, of North Yorkshire, it was stated in the July letter that:

*The polling commissioned by district councils did not show a clear outcome of informed opinion.*

Nothing was said as to why opinion was 'informed' in that county and there was nothing in the November document to enlighten one.

### Conclusion

The preceding account of the material in the November summary of consultation responses confirms conclusions reached in preceding Chapters, that the decision process was inconsistent, relying on the movement of goalposts and on the use of selective and misleading information. Indeed, the present chapter shows that the decisions are inexplicable when judged against the avowed criteria, with the 'evidence' selected to suit decisions evidently taken on other grounds.

These conclusions are themselves fully confirmed by the attitude of the Government to the consultation responses, as articulated by Baroness Andrews:

> *We deliberately did not look for public support, we did not require local referendums, and we did not make this a test of public opinion … However, we thought that there needed to be sufficient confidence about the new council among … the public sector … [and] the business community.*

But, in addition:

> *There also needed to be a level of confidence about improvements among local people.*

And:

> *I also said at the beginning that we never intended this to be a popular referendum. … You tap into emotion and loyalty, which are perfectly valid, but perhaps that is not what you should be looking for in introducing a change of this sort, when you need to deliver better local government and better services.* (Hansard 21 February 2008, cols GC26, 27, 46 and 47.)

In this contorted way, the Government made clear its distrust of public opinion but the Baroness went considerably further during the House of Lords debate on the Order to create a Cheshire unitary authority:

> *Let me be clear about what the definition of 'broad cross section of support' actually means, as set out in the original invitation. It is, essentially, about whether the new unitary authority genuinely meets its objectives and will work for local people.* (Hansard 4 March 2008, col. 1032.)

The ingredient that seems to be entirely lacking is the idea that people need to be persuaded before action is taken, instead of merely being expected to be grateful to an all-wise Government after it has imposed its will.

No doubt the re-definition of 'broad cross section of support' would appeal to Humpty Dumpty.

# 6

# Legal challenge by Shrewsbury and Congleton

The fact that judicial review proceedings were running parallel with the LGR process has been mentioned and now is the time to explain what was going on and what was at stake. There were in fact two cases, the more significant being discussed in this chapter; the Bedfordshire case is the subject of Chapter 7.

Two districts, Shrewsbury & Atcham in Shropshire and Congleton in Cheshire, opposing unitary proposals in their respective counties, separately initiated proceedings, the primary allegation being that the Secretary of State had exceeded her powers. These two applications became a joint action, with the support of a significant number of other districts, though they were not formally parties to it. In addition, a number of authorities considered taking judicial steps of their own but these did not proceed pending the outcome of the Shrewsbury/Congleton initiative. The application took on some of the characteristics of a class action, the purpose of which was to stop the LGR process.

The judicial review proceedings initiated by Shrewsbury and Congleton had major potential implications for the LGR process but their significance goes much wider because the fundamental issue at stake was the extent of the powers that can legitimately be exercised by the Government – the sources of power, and the limitations. At the heart of the proceedings was the extent to which Government can rely upon what is generally called Common Law. Therefore, the issues were, and remain, extremely important for the way in which the country is governed, even though the two districts lost their case.

## Some general matters

Table 6.1 sets out the key dates of the judicial process. Despite agreement of the parties that expedition was important, the proceedings lasted for most of the period occupied by the LGR. The High Court heard the case in September 2007 and Mr Justice Underhill's judgment became available in October ([2007] EWHC 2279 (ADMIN)). He dismissed the application but gave leave to appeal and this hearing was in January 2008. The three Court of Appeal judges, Lord Justices Carnwath, Richards and Waller, endorsed the conclusion reached in the High Court, their judgment being handed down in March 2008 ([1487] EWCA Civ).

### Table 6.1
Shrewsbury and Congleton judicial review proceedings, key dates

| Proceedings issued: | Shrewsbury | 20 April 2007 |
|---|---|---|
| | Congleton | 25 May 2007 |
| Order for the two cases to be heard together | | 5 June 2007 |
| Permission granted to proceed | | 18 June 2007 |
| High court hearing | | 12-14 September 2007 |
| Judgment, with leave to appeal. | | |
| [2007] EWHC 2279 (ADMIN) | | 10 October 2007 |
| Appeal hearing | | 28-30 January 2008 |
| Judgment. [148] EWCA Civ | | 4 March 2008 |

Because the case went to appeal, there is a matter of terminology to clarify. In the High Court, the parties were the Applicants (the districts) and the Defendant (the Secretary of State), but in the Court of Appeal the same parties were respectively the Appellants and the Respondent. To be legally correct, our discussion should use the terms appropriate for the two courts but this could be confusing for those unfamiliar with legal conventions. We have chosen to refer to the two parties as the Districts and as the Secretary of State, in the belief that this is the most easily understood way to proceed. The court to which reference is being made is identified where this is relevant. Shropshire CC was represented throughout as an interested party.

By the time that the appeal judgment was delivered on 4 March 2008, implementation Orders for the five unitary counties had completed the parliamentary process; the Order to create two unitary authorities in Cheshire was debated in the House of Lords, and passed, just a few hours after the judgment was published; and the Order to implement two unitary authorities in Bedfordshire was published on 6 March.

Because the litigation was proceeding in parallel with the LGR, there was a problem regarding the grounds on which the action was brought. When the proceedings were initiated, the March letters had been published, identifying the proposals that went forward for consultation and those which did not, and the March-June consultation was progressing; the LGR was at a fairly early stage. However, at the time of the High Court hearing in September, the July decision letters had been dispatched. Mr Arden QC, acting for the Districts, asked for the July letters to be included in the case, a request to which the Secretary of State and the court agreed. This had been arranged in good time, so that the July decisions were fully incorporated into the High Court proceedings. There was a similar problem when the Court of Appeal sat in January 2008, because the December announcements had been made and letters dispatched, but on this occasion Mr Arden sought to have them excluded. It was only towards the end of the second day's hearing that the court insisted on their inclusion, with the details of how this was to be done being settled at the start of the third and final day. Any written submissions about the December letters were to be with the court no later than a week after the hearing ended. The effect of this procedural detail was to limit discussion about the December letters during the hearing, and to limit what was brought to the attention of the court in writing.

### The grounds on which the judicial review was brought

Expressed in non-technical terms, the three grounds on which the Districts brought the case against the Secretary of State were:

1.  Vires. That the Secretary of State did not have the power to proceed in the way that she was doing/had done.

2.  That she had ignored her own criteria, in that she was not entitled to find that the proposals met the 'broad cross section of support' criterion.

3.  That she had acted unfairly in the consultation process, particularly because the DCLG's LGR web-page did not include any links to web-pages with material that was critical of the proposals.

The first of these grounds was the most fundamental, and the one with wider constitutional significance.

For convenience, the three grounds are treated separately below, under the headings used by Underhill J in his October 2007 High Court judgment.

### Ground 1. Vires. Power to act

The issue at stake was that of defining the limits to the powers of the Government to take action. It was common ground that, at the time of the action and the main stages of the LGR, the extant legal framework for reorganising local government in England was the 1992 Act as amended. It was also common ground that, whatever decisions the Secretary of State came to, she could not proceed to implementation until the Local Government and Public Involvement in Health Bill had been enacted. The central issue was the nature of the powers, if any, under which the Secretary of State could initiate the review process and follow it through to the point of reaching decisions; whether decisions published in March and July constituted final decisions; and what was the relationship between the July decisions and the ostensibly final ones announced in December?

In the absence of specific statutory provisions for proceeding in the manner adopted, Mr Eadie, acting for the Secretary of State, initially relied upon Crown prerogative as the basis for her authority to initiate the LGR and to follow through thereon but resiled from this position to the alternative argument, that she had the power to undertake 'governmental business' under Common Law. It became accepted ground between the parties that Crown prerogative powers are now treated narrowly, confined to such matters as the power to declare war, to grant pardons and to confer honours. Under Common Law, Mr Eadie argued, the Secretary of State may do anything that is not specifically prohibited in law, as if she were a private citizen. The thinking behind this position may be illustrated in the following way.

The level of national taxes is set by Parliament, with changes usually included in the annual Finance Act. With the rate for taxes set in this manner, there is no explicit provision to employ the staff needed to collect the sums due and to purchase the office necessities for this process, such as paper clips. These activities are necessary incidentals to the statutory provisions, and do not require specific legislation. Applied to the matter in hand, Mr Eadie argued that the Government had the right and the power to take action preparatory to legislative changes, and that this is in fact something that is going on all the time. Furthermore, he argued, the process initiated in October 2006 was in preparation for the legislative changes enshrined in the Bill that became the 2007 Act.

It was agreed that the Government certainly has the power to initiate discussions about making legislative changes, including the publication of White Papers. However, in this case, Mr Arden argued, the consultations were not about whether and how to change the legislative framework, but over the implementation of provisions in a Bill when it became an Act. The Secretary of State's argument was that the invitation to submit proposals, and the consultation thereon, were legitimate preparations for taking decisions once the Bill had been enacted. At no point did Mr Eadie claim that she could take final decisions before the Bill became law. Opposing this position on behalf of the Districts, Mr Arden argued that the March refusals to proceed with ten proposals were in fact final decisions, and that the 'minded to' decisions announced in July were also final, at least for the six proposals that were subsequently to be implemented by Order, including proposals for Cheshire and Shropshire.

Had the DCLG merely been considering whether to refer particular proposals to the Boundary Committee for their consideration, there would not have been an issue if the outcome had been decisions either to refer or not to refer the area in question to the Boundary Committee, with no comments made on the merits or otherwise of specific proposals. On the other hand, if the Secretary of State had followed up the letters dispatched in July 2007 by laying Orders before Parliament while the Bill was still being considered, it would have been clear-cut that she had acted unlawfully.

The problem was that the Secretary of State had started the whole process in October 2006 by announcing the intention to reach final conclusions in July 2007, maintaining that position into April 2008, while the letters dispatched in July conveyed decisions in the form of 'minded to' implement or not implement. In addition, the Bill, and then the Act, contained provisions retrospectively to endorse the issuing of invitations and consultations thereon. So where was the limit to the power of the Secretary of State to use Common Law for what she had done?

In his October High Court judgment, Underhill J held that the 1992 Act (as amended) did not cover the entire relevant field relating to procedures for structural change of local government. He also held that preparatory work for a change in legislation is a permissible activity for Government, applying generally and also in this case. In addition, he argued, it is impossible to define limits to such preparation. On this basis, Underhill J concluded that the Secretary of State was not precluded from acting as she had. Recording Mr Arden's submission on behalf of the Districts, 'that the decisions recorded in the letters of 25 July 2007 were in substance final decisions, contingent only on the passage of the Bill' he went on to say:

> *It seems to me that once it be conceded that in principle preparatory work of this kind may be lawful it is impossible to define meaningful boundaries of the kind necessary to Mr Arden's submission. In my judgment such work will only cease to be lawful at the point at which the Minister purports to exercise actual governmental authority in a manner inconsistent with the existing statutory regime* (High Court, para. 21).

Carnwath LJ wrote the lead judgment for the Court of Appeal and came to a different conclusion from Underhill J:

> *In conclusion, I generally support the reasoning and conclusions of the judge. As I have made clear, I have more concerns than him about the extent to which a wholly non-statutory procedure has been used to prepare the way for decisions, in an area which is accepted as the province of the legislature. I have also pointed out the potential risks of such a course. I understand that one purpose was to limit the period of uncertainty accompanying structural change. But it seems to me a constitutional principle of some importance that local authorities should be able to rely on the safeguards of a statutory framework for the processes leading to decisions of this importance. However, in the end, I find it impossible to avoid the conclusion that Parliament has (if only retrospectively) given its stamp of approval to the procedure in this case, and there is no evidence that the authorities have been prejudiced in presenting their opposition.* (Court of Appeal, para. 70.)

Richards LJ disagreed with Carnwath LJ on two matters:

> *I agree with Carnwath LJ's conclusions and with much of his reasoning. I do not, however, share his reservations about the extent of the common law powers of the Crown ... Like Underhill J, I do not read the 1992 Act as preventing the taking of action by Ministers by way of preparation for the introduction of a different statutory regime* (Court of Appeal paras 72 and 75).

However, Waller LJ sympathised with the views of Carnwath LJ about limits to the powers of Government:

*I instinctively favour some constraint on the powers* [of the Government] *by reference to the duty to act only for the public benefit but until one has actual facts by reference to which the matter can be fully tested, it is unwise to say more.*

And:

*The second area where there is a difference of opinion relates to the question whether the Government were acting inconsistently with the 1992 Act. I would agree with Carnwath LJ's view on this aspect. One reason I have for supporting his view is that it seems to me that the action being taken was in an area which the 1992 Act was designed to cover. The action was not simply preliminary to bringing in an Act to change the 1992 Act with the intention thereafter of acting under a new statutory scheme. The action being taken was to treat the 1992 scheme as having already been repealed.* (Court of Appeal, paras. 81 and 82.)

Two of the Appeal Court judges considered that the Government had indeed been acting in a manner contrary to the 1992 Act and beyond the limits of their powers, and to this extent supported the submission of Mr Arden for the Districts. Nevertheless, all three were unanimous in rejecting the appeal. Why?

Their judgment turned on the status of the December letters. Mr Arden argued the decisions then announced amounted to the decisions taken in July, and that those decisions were null because the Secretary of State had no power to take them. On the other hand, Mr Eadie for the Secretary of State, did not rely on any principle of ratification, arguing that they were new decisions taken after the 2007 Act commenced. On this matter, Carnwath LJ had this to say (Court of Appeal, para. 67):

*The overwhelming difficulty Mr Arden faces in making that submission is in the evidence. On the unchallenged evidence of Mr Rowsell for the Secretary of State, there was in December a genuine reconsideration of the merits of the two proposals now in issue. If that was not clear from other documents, it is put beyond doubt by his sixth witness statement filed in response to this allegation. He explains the steps taken following the decision in July 2007, including meetings with the affected authorities, and consideration of new representations. As to the decisions taken in December, following commencement of the Act, he says:*

*'The Secretary of State decided that in all the circumstances, the appropriate course when taking these decisions would be to judge the 26 proposals against the criteria (which now had the status of guidance under section 3(5) of the Act as to*

*what a proposal should seek to achieve). It was on this basis, having considered the factors and options set out to her, including all of the additional material that she had received after 25 July 2007 ... that the Secretary of State took her decisions ...'*

Mr Rowsell was the senior civil servant overseeing the LGR. His witness statement, submitted after the court had risen, went unchallenged. Faced with this uncontested evidence, the three judges could arrive at only one conclusion, that there had been full reconsideration of all the proposals in November/December 2007. Consequently, because the Act had commenced, and had given statutory endorsement for the actions taken during the LGR, the December decisions were lawful, and the Districts' case had to be rejected.

The decision by Mr Arden to try to exclude the December letters had left him with minimal opportunity to contest Mr Rowsell's witness statement. Had there been prior preparation about the December letters, some telling points could have been made to counter Mr Rowsell's claim.

### Grounds for challenging the claim that there was a full re-consideration
#### *The two-unitary option for Cheshire*

Although the decision about Cheshire has already been scrutinised, we need to re-consider the matter in the light of the Appeal Court judgment, because it probably provides the strongest ground for believing that the re-assessment undertaken by the Secretary of State cannot have been as thorough as was claimed.

The letter to Chester City Council and the districts supporting two unitary councils, dated 18 December, referred to the 25 July letter, noting that it was then thought the two competing proposals would meet the criteria. However:

> *On balance, the Secretary of State judged that your two-unitary proposal for Cheshire would deliver to a greater extent the long-term outcomes specified by the criteria around strategic leadership, neighbourhood empowerment and <u>value for money and equity on public services</u>. This is the process that we set out in the consultation document 'Means for Prioritising Proposals', issued in June 2007.*

Missing from the December letter was any mention of the concern expressed in July about the risks on the Affordability criterion for the two unitary councils; nor was there any mention of the request for further work to be done on the financial case. Despite this oversight, the December letter stated that the further representations had been considered, confirmed the July 'minded to' letters about both unitary proposals and then continued:

> *The Secretary of State remains of the view that, on balance, your proposal for a two-unitary Cheshire will deliver to a greater extent the long-term outcomes specified by the criteria around strategic leadership, neighbourhood empowerment and value for money and equity on public services. She accordingly intends to implement your proposal by order made under section 7 of the Local Government and Public Involvement in Health Act 2007.*

The December letter contained no discussion of the merits of the two competing unitary proposals on the criteria of Affordability and Support, having reduced the choice to the balance of advantage on just three criteria, on which basis stating that the two-unitary option was to be preferred to the single council 'on balance'. This does not seem to be a complete evaluation of all five criteria, such as one would expect had there been the thorough re-assessment that was claimed took place after 1 November, and these doubts are reinforced by another feature of the 18 December letter.

Having stated the assessment and decision noted above, the letter then undermined what had just been said, because the Secretary of State:

> *Noted* [that], *although the potential economies of scale would be larger for a single unitary, this needed to be balanced against the other criteria, where her judgment was that the single authority would deliver less effective strategic leadership and community and neighbourhood empowerment.*

And:

> *In relation to Value for money* ...[she] *has concluded that, on balance, a single Cheshire unitary would be reasonably likely to achieve to a greater extent the outcomes specified by this criterion.*

The contradiction within the letter about the Value for money criterion indicates that this letter cannot have been written on the basis of a careful review of all the material. Furthermore, if a single unitary council would perform better on Value for money than two councils, it follows that the single unitary would also perform better on the Affordability criterion, but there was no discussion of this in the letter. Finally, re-evaluation of the Support criterion would have shown that opinion strongly favoured one council in preference to two. On three out of the five criteria, a single unitary council was to be preferred, but that is not the impression conveyed by the December letter. The structure and content of the letter are inconsistent with Mr Rowsell's claim that everything was reviewed after the commencement of the 2007 Act.

### The December decisions more generally

If the decisions announced in December were genuinely independent assessments, why did Mr Healey announce the decisions by confirming the July 'minded to' decisions? A proper re-assessment would have been reported by stating for each criterion that the proposal had passed the threshold of acceptability, stating the over-all conclusion and then pointing out that this confirmed the 'minded to' decision. Recollect that the July letters were structured around criteria in an order that differed from the original order and with wording for the individual criteria that was not an exact replica of the originals. It is difficult to accept that there had been a genuinely new decision process.

### March letters of refusal

Mr Arden contended that the letters sent to authorities in March, saying that their proposals, numbering ten altogether, would not proceed to consultation, amounted to final decisions, citing a document issued in April by the DCLG, 'Frequently Asked Questions'. This document made it clear that the door had been closed on the ten proposals, with no appeal against the decisions. However, there was a fatal problem for Mr Arden, because one of the ten rejected proposals was in fact re-considered by the DCLG. This was the proposal for a unitary authority to cover the whole of Bedfordshire other than Bedford BC. When the July letters were issued, the Department stated that it was minded to implement Bedford's proposal but that this would need a unitary council for the remainder of the county, for which an invitation would be issued (see Chapter 7).

With that important exception, there can be little doubt that the decision in March for the other nine rejected cases was the substantive decision, as made clear in December by Mr Healey, probably quite unintentionally. It will be recollected (p. 28) that his statement to Parliament on 5 December 2007 included words to the effect that the Secretary of State, having considered all the material available, including additional material received since July 2007, was confirming her July 'minded to' letters in all cases except Exeter and Ipswich. The statement then went on to say: 'Further, the Secretary of State has decided to take no action on the 14 unitary proposals listed' below. Read carefully, the four counties for which 'minded to' letters of rejection had been sent out in July were included in this list of fourteen; these four were therefore covered by the general observation relating to all the 'minded to' letters. There was no separate statement that the Secretary of State had 'considered all the information and representations now available to her …' in respect of the proposals rejected in March. In any case, even if there had been further consideration of these cases, there would have been little or nothing in the way of additional material since March because of the DCLG's categorical position that the matter had been closed. Any 're-consideration' would have been nothing other than token.

There is an additional reason for stating that a final decision had been taken in March to reject bids that were not taken forward for consultation. According to the invitation document issued in October 2006, the Government did not expect to implement more than eight proposals, for the following reason. Structural change implies transition costs, costs that have to be incurred before the claimed savings can begin to accrue. Consequently, if there were a sizeable number of proposals being implemented simultaneously, there would be an identifiable increase, in the short term, in aggregate public expenditure. The Government took the view that, to stay within the established rules for public finances, the expenditure impact of reorganisation had to be controlled by limiting the maximum number of proposals that could go forward. The reasoning is difficult to accept, given the scale of total public spending and of the national debt, about £540 billion net in March 2008, not including Northern Rock liabilities amounting to about £100 billion gross. Nevertheless, a numerical limit was set for the maximum number of new unitary councils, and procedures were put in place to prioritise bids if there were a danger of the financial envelope being breached.

This approach became relevant for the rejections in the following way. Sixteen proposals went forward for consultation, including competing proposals in three cases – Bedfordshire, Cheshire and Northumberland – meaning that thirteen was the maximum number of proposals that could conceivably be implemented. The DCLG (2007b) issued a document in June about the process for prioritising proposals should the prospective number of successful proposals exceed the limit that had been set. In fact, with a maximum of nine proposals going forward in July, the prioritisation that had been envisaged was not necessary.

The implication is clear. At the time decisions were being taken in July, the financial constraint precluded any addition to the number of contenders, effectively locking the door that had been closed in March. Viewed in this light, there was no room, and never had been any room, for substantive re-consideration of nine March rejection decisions. Although the Government would like it to be thought that rejection decisions were finally taken after 1 November 2007, the reality is that 're-consideration' had been pre-empted; at that point in time, there was no room for discretion to alter the earlier decision with respect to the nine cases.

### July 'minded to' letters: five successful counties

There were five counties for which the Secretary of State was, in July, 'minded to' implement single unitaries, which proposals were confirmed in December when the statutory powers had come into existence. For each of these five proposals, the term used in July was 'minded to implement', and not 'minded to decide'. This distinction may seem small, even trivial, but the implication is that the Secretary of State had come to a conclusion and would implement the proposal 'if and when the Local Government and Public Involvement in Health Bill is enacted'. This implication was confirmed by two actions by the DCLG and noted by the Court of Appeal.

Following the July letters, the Department encouraged the local authorities in August to establish joint implementation committees to begin preparatory work, and they were set up. If there had been a genuine possibility that the July decisions were provisional, it would have been wrong for the Department to prompt local authorities to use resources for a project that had a serious possibility of not being confirmed once the Bill was enacted. Indeed, at the Appeal Court hearing, Shropshire CC claimed that they had incurred substantial costs preparing for a unitary county and argued that it would be wrong to quash the decision because of the waste of public money this would involve. In other words, Shropshire had acted in good faith on the understanding that the July decision was final, subject only to the Bill being passed with the relevant clauses intact.

The second matter is the drafting of the Orders that would be laid before Parliament to implement unitary proposals. Drafts were circulating in both Cornwall and Co. Durham by 22 October, before the 2007

Act came into force on 1 November. The DCLG was acting as if the final decision had been taken and was anxious to get on with the job. If there had been a genuine possibility that the July decisions would be altered, then devoting resources to the draft Orders, and expecting local authorities to do so as well, would have been irresponsible. If, on the other hand, the actual decision had been taken, then the claim by the Department that all the material available had been reviewed and fresh decisions reached was not true. Neither possibility inspires confidence in the DCLG.

### Some other matters relevant to Ground 1

Some additional matters relating to Ground 1 deserve to be mentioned. The Appeal Court judges were exercised by the decision of the Secretary of State to proceed as if the 1992 Act had been repealed and Carnwath LJ emphasised this concern in two ways. He quoted some text from the *Regulatory Impact Assessment* that accompanied the Bill which became the 2007 Act, explaining that the 1992 Act did not provide for local authorities to initiate structural change, going on to say:

> *The option of 'using the present legislation and asking the Electoral Commission for advice' had been rejected because — 'it has never been the intention to use the Electoral Commission in this way. At the time of the transfer of the Local Government Commission to the Electoral Commission it was clearly stated that the "Electoral Commission would not be asked to conduct any wholesale review of local government". As set out above experience shows that such a review would be disproportionately lengthy, divisive and expensive.'* (Court of Appeal, para. 9.)

The judge did not comment on this observation. However, the LGR was not a wholesale review. Therefore, by implication, the judge was pointing out that there was no obvious reason for declining to use the 1992 Act as the mechanism for initiating structural change.

One of the reasons given by Underhill J for arguing that the Secretary of State had been acting within her powers was set out as follows:

> *Although the Secretary of State was indeed very active in relation to the proposals, and expended significant resources in promoting and considering them, she at no time purported to exercise any authority over any other person (natural or artificial)* (High Court, para. 19).

That claim runs counter to the fact that the Secretary of State had threatened she would compel local authorities to cooperate in the preparation of unitary proposals if they did not do so voluntarily (DCLG 2006, para. 4.22), and Carnwath LJ made it clear that he did not agree with Underhill J:

> *I have noted the Secretary of State's threat … to use powers under section 230 of the Local Government Act 1972. That requires authorities to respond to requests for information 'with respect to their functions'. In the course of argument I raised the question what 'functions' of the Boroughs were engaged. The only answer, as I understood it, was a reference to the general powers of a local authority (under section 2 of the Local Government Act 2000), to do anything which 'they consider' likely to achieve the promotion of the economic and social well-being of their area. At first sight it seems somewhat artificial to read that as enabling the Secretary of State to compel participation in a non-statutory process with which the authorities fundamentally disagree and which would lead to their destruction.*
> (Court of Appeal, para. 60.)

### Some matters that did not come to the attention of the Courts

An issue not mentioned by the Appeal Court judges reinforces the reasons for concern about the LGR process. When the Bill that became the 2007 Act was published, it provided that the Secretary of State 'may invite or direct any principal authority' to make unitary proposals. This provision survived into the Act (Section 3(1)(b)), although the power of direction lapsed on 25 January 2008. No direction was issued, but the Bill contained a threat that authority might be exercised by direction over councils to undertake something that they did not wish to do. This makes nonsense of the claim, going back to 2006 and repeated by Ministers thereafter, that it was entirely up to councils whether they formulated proposals.

When Parliament was told in July that the Secretary of State was 'minded to' implement nine proposals for unitary structures, Mr Healey's written statement said:

> *These new unitaries, as they move towards implementation … Implementing Bedford borough's proposal means that we must consider the future local government structures for the remaining county area …* (Hansard 25 July 2007, col. 69WS.)

On the same day, 25 July, the Department issued a press release under the title 'Healey announces nine successful unitary proposals'. These words implied that decisions had been taken and that it was merely a matter of waiting for the 2007 Act before implementation.

On the first day of the High Court hearing, 12 September 2007, the DCLG issued an invitation for expressions of interest in conducting research on new unitary and Pathfinder councils. This invitation envisaged that the research would examine 'the effectiveness of the new unitary authorities' and gave a timetable as follows:

| | |
|---|---|
| September 2007 | Expressions of interest. |
| Mid/end October 2007 | Invitations to tender issued. |
| December 2007 | Contract awarded. |
| January 2008 | Project commences. |

It is difficult to imagine this timetable being feasible unless the Department, at that time, thought final decisions had been taken which could be divulged to bidders to enable them to make realistic proposals. Those decisions would have been taken before the 2007 Act commenced on 1 November.

On 31 January 2008, the day after the Appeal Court hearing concluded, the Order to implement two unitary councils in Cheshire was laid, along with the customary Explanatory Memorandum. This Memorandum (para. 7.16) recorded that the Secretary of State had decided to confirm her July 'minded to' letter, repeating the conclusion that this bid was better than a single council on the three criteria identified in the letter and confirmed to Parliament on 18 December 2007. Attached to the Memorandum as Annex B was the verbatim text of the 25 July letter sent to Chester and the councils supporting the two unitary proposal, not the letter sent on 18 December. The terms of the July letter differed from the December one. It would appear that Members of Parliament were not shown the December letter because of the direct contradiction contained therein about Value for money. Including the July letter, it would seem, implied that it was more significant than the Government was willing to admit in court.

Yet other information became available too late to be brought to the attention of the Appeal Court. The Order to implement two unitary councils in Bedfordshire was not laid until 6 March 2008. When this

Order was debated in the House of Lords Grand Committee, Baroness Andrews, for the Government, explained the timetable for this proposal and why the decision had only recently been taken, using the 'minded to' letter of 25 July 2007 as her starting point. That letter had made it clear that the Government wished to proceed with a unitary Bedford but for this to happen there would have to be a satisfactory unitary proposal for the county outside the town. For this purpose, an invitation would be issued, but this was not done until 19 November 2007:

> *We could not have issued that earlier for two reasons. First, in the light of several challenges brought by councils against the Secretary of State in relation to the 'minded to' decisions and the first pre-statutory invitation, it was appropriate to wait for the Local Government and Public Involvement in Health Act 2007 to receive the Royal Assent. ...* (Hansard 25 March 2008, col. GC 102.)

Despite everything else, it would appear that the Government had recognised that it was on unsafe ground in acting prior to 1 November as if the 2007 Act were in force.

On the other hand, the ambivalence of the Government's position was demonstrated by the timetable that was set for the submission of the proposal for which the November invitation was issued:

> *We gave councils four weeks to respond to that because we wanted to minimise the period of uncertainty ... We also made clear in July that we were going to issue a further invitation for the remainder of Bedfordshire, so councils had an extensive opportunity to get together to do the preparatory work.* (Hansard 25 March 2008, col. GC 102.)

In other words, from July, councils were to assume that Bedford would become a unitary authority and there would be a unitary structure for the rest of the county; they were expected to have been working on the proposal long before the 2007 Act commenced.

### Conclusions on Ground 1.

There is no doubt that the Appeal Court judges considered that 'local authorities should be able to rely on the safeguards of a statutory framework for the processes leading to decisions of this importance' (Court of Appeal, para. 0). Consequently, they were unhappy with the way in which the Secretary of State had proceeded, acting as if the 1992 Act had been repealed.

The problem was that when the Appeal Court sat, the Local Government Act 2007 had been passed, Mr Rowsell had submitted a Witness Statement to the effect that there had been a full re-consideration of all the unitary proposals after the commencement of the Act, and that Statement had not been contested. Given these circumstances, there were no legal grounds on which the judges could find for the Districts. Whether the outcome would have been any different had the December letters been brought into the proceedings earlier than was the case is impossible to say, but there were grounds for a strong challenge as to the facts about a full re-consideration of the proposals and therefore the genuineness of the 'decisions' taken after 1 November 2007.

There is a sense that this case illustrates the old saying that 'justice delayed is justice denied'. However, what might have happened if the legal process had been completed at an earlier point in the LGR is a matter for speculation.

## Ground 2. Broad cross-section of support

At the appeal hearing, there was substantial discussion about the following general issue. It was agreed by the parties that the terms of the criteria had been modified in some degree during the course of the LGR, something that has been discussed in Chapter 2. If we focus on the Support criterion, the change was from a test requiring that a broad cross section of support be demonstrated for a proposal before it was adopted to a test about the probability of that support being forthcoming after a proposal had been implemented. Mr Arden for the Districts argued that the post hoc test was not appropriate. Mr Eadie for the Secretary of State claimed that she was fully entitled to change the criteria during the LGR process.

The argument of principle against Mr Eadie was framed in terms of 'legitimate expectation', that the rules of the process having been established at the beginning it was not appropriate to change them part way except for good reasons that could be accepted by those affected. As a general principle, it would seem impossible for public life to be conducted justly and efficiently if the relevant rules of engagement can be changed at the will of ministers part-way through a specified process.

The Appeal Court judges found against Mr Arden on this point, apparently because the process adopted by the Secretary of State did not fall within a specific statutory framework:

*It is well-established that a promise by a public authority to follow a particular procedure may give rise to an enforceable 'legitimate expectation'. However, outside a specific statutory framework, such a procedural expectation is not set in stone. It may be varied or withdrawn, at least so long as due notice is given, and no procedural prejudice is suffered.* (Court of Appeal, para. 40.)

The judges found that there had been no 'procedural prejudice'. Although 'It would have seemed as though the referee were moving the goalposts', there was no legal peg available on which to hang the argument about 'legitimate expectation', because the LGR was outwith the existing relevant statutory framework.

From a lay perspective, the implication of this finding is that, where the Government is acting outside the existing relevant statutory framework, as for the LGR, the concept of 'legitimate expectation' has less force than when the actions are within the statutory envelope. This seems to be a reason for ensuring that statutes are honoured by their observance, and confirms the need for the limits to the power of the Government to be defined.

### Ground 3. The Department's web-page

The basic issue under this heading was one of fairness, in that the DCLG's web-page for the LGR included links to the local authorities proposing structural change but no links to web-pages with critical material, despite requests from some local authorities. Mr Eadie defended this arrangement on the grounds that there was no duty on the DCLG to provide such links, and that the number might be intolerably large. At the September hearing, Underhill J was acerbic about the failure to provide direct links to the web-pages of the local authorities in affected areas that were in opposition to proposals. However, in his judgment he concluded as follows:

*Even if it could be criticised as ungenerous, the omission could not possibly be regarded as a sufficiently substantial failing to justify treating the consultation as inadequate or the resulting decisions as unlawful* (High Court, para. 38).

At the appeal hearing, Mr Arden conceded that he could offer no proof that the consultation had been prejudiced and the Court of Appeal concurred with Underhill J.

## Implications of the legal challenge

The timetable for the LGR was not affected by the case brought by Shrewsbury and Congleton, nor was its outcome. Viewed narrowly, it could be said that a considerable amount of public money was wasted, but that narrow view would be a mistake. By going to court, the districts have revealed some troubling aspects of the LGR. Exposed for everyone to see is the unhappiness of the Appeal Court judges that the Secretary of State had acted as if the Local Government Act 1992 had been repealed. They took the view that local authorities should have been able to rely on the safeguards of the existing statutory framework.

It appears that this lesson has been lost on the Government. During a debate on the Order to implement two unitary councils in Bedford-shire, Baroness Andrews noted the judicial review challenge mounted by Bedfordshire CC about the 25 July letters for that county, stating that any problems there might be had been superseded by the 2007 Act:

> *This reasoning reflects the Court of Appeal's conclusion in the related Shrewsbury and Congleton case that decisions or actions made in advance of the orders coming into force under the Act were no more than preparatory steps* ... (Hansard 25 March 2008, col. GC 105).

This statement is wrong for two reasons. The Appeal Court judges were exercised by the actions taken before the 2007 Act commenced; actions taken after 1 November were regarded as legal. On this issue, Baroness Andrews' statement was inaccurate. Second, and far more important, the judges did not accept that actions before 1 November 'were no more than preparatory steps'. The judgment handed down makes it clear that the Government went far beyond 'preparatory steps'; the DCLG had acted as if the Act were in force when it was not. The statement was a disingenuous attempt to re-write the case history.

Acting as it did with the LGR, the Government was chipping away at the concept of the rule of law and the protections that statutes provide. There was arrogation of power. We hope that there will be a test case that will serve to define with some precision what the powers of Government are. Meantime, we are concerned that the way may have been opened for other freedoms and protections accorded by statute to be eroded by non-statutory means. If the particular case has revealed nothing else, it is that the rule of law is under threat, a matter that should be of urgent concern for all citizens, in all walks of life, who value the concept of freedom under the law.

# 7

# Legal challenge by
# Bedfordshire

Bedfordshire county council lost its judicial review application, the judgment on the case being published on 4 April 2008 ([2008] EWHC 628 (Admin.)). Notice had been given by Bedfordshire of its intention to seek a judicial review, in the form of a pre-action protocol letter to the Secretary of State dated 15 August 2007, to which there had been no reply by the time the application was filed on 12 October. The hearing on 22 February 2008 was a permission hearing, and the judgment was a refusal of permission for a judicial review. In other words, the case did not proceed to a full hearing. The council decided not to appeal.

The case was distinct from the case brought by Shrewsbury and Congleton and needs to be considered for the specific issues raised. There was no allegation that the Secretary of State had acted outwith her statutory powers, as in the Shrewsbury and Congleton application. Instead, Bedfordshire's case was that the Secretary of State had contravened the rules for the LGR that she had laid down. The matters lying at the heart of Bedfordshire CC's case revolved around the July 'minded to' letters sent to the county and to Bedford BC, the timetable originally established for the LGR and the criteria to be applied. Specifically, the county objected to the Secretary of State's intention to invite a revised unitary proposal for the county outside Bedford, contending that the only proposals that should be considered were their own for a single unitary county and Bedford's, and that Bedford's had failed on the Affordability criterion.

The original timetable set by the DCLG was for final decisions to be taken in July 2007 (Table 2.1). Leading up to those decisions, there would be consultation on the proposals that, in the judgement of the Department in March, met all five criteria. No further action would be taken on proposals failing to meet all five tests (DCLG 2006b). When the March announcement was made that sixteen proposals would go forward, a document was published re-affirming the original timetable and confirming that only proposals that had met the five criteria were going forward for consultation (DCLG 2007c). During the consultation period March-June 2007, the business case could be 'further developed' for the sixteen proposals. These procedural rules had been set out in a manner that the county claimed provided an 'exhaustive', i.e., complete, specification of how matters would be handled.

Three proposals for Bedfordshire had been submitted in January, of which one failed to meet four of the five criteria, passing only on the level of Support, this being the proposal from Mid and South Bedfordshire for a unitary authority covering the whole of the county outside Bedford. Bedford's bid assumed a unitary council for the remainder of the county and included costings on that basis, but did not submit a detailed proposal for this assumed council. However, during the consultation period, further work was done on the rejected Mid/South Bedfordshire proposal, with the result that a new document was prepared which was submitted by Bedford as Section 8 of its supplementary submission in June 2007. The foreword to this document, by the leaders of the two districts, claimed that the January submission was not a formal proposal but instead complementary to the Bedford proposal, and that the new submission had been prepared following meetings with the Minister for Local Government and Community Cohesion and his team. It is also understood that a joint proposal for Mid/South Bedfordshire was submitted direct to the DCLG on 21 June.

In July, the DCLG announced that the Bedford proposal for a unitary city had been accepted on five criteria but had asked for further work to be done on the Affordability criterion. The county argued in its legal submission that the request for further work on the Affordability criterion meant that the proposal had failed to meet all five criteria and should not have been allowed to remain in contention; and that the Secretary of State had acted irrationally. They also argued that the timetable had allowed for further work to be done on the business case during the March-June consultation period but had made no provision for additional work after the consultation deadline. Finally, because the

Mid/South Bedfordshire proposal had been rejected in March, the county argued that it was wrong for the Secretary of State to conclude in July that an invitation would be issued for a new proposal. In summary terms, these were the grounds on which the county council alleged that the Secretary of State had broken her own 'exhaustive' statement of how the LGR would be handled, in effect moving the goalposts and thereby disregarding legitimate expectation.

## The judgment

By the time of the hearing, the 2007 Act had commenced. Consequently, it is not surprising that the application failed, because the Act gave retrospective authority for everything the Secretary of State had done by way of issuing invitations and undertaking consultations in anticipation of decisions to be taken after 1 November 2007. As the Appeal Court noted, because there was no statutory peg for the criteria and timetable, the Secretary of State had full discretion to make changes as the LGR process unfolded. If the judgment by Sir Robin Auld had left matters there, the case would not have been remarkable, although troubling for its confirmation of the weakness of 'legitimate expectation' when the Government acts outside statute law. However, the manner in which the judgment was constructed amounted to a curious re-writing of history.

In the summary of the background to the case, Sir Robin Auld acknowledged that he was drawing on the skeleton argument submitted on behalf of the Secretary of State, including excerpts from July 'minded to' letters which, it will be remembered, referred to decisions to implement or not implement proposals. Embedded in the background history, the judge referred to the 25 July announcement about Bedford's proposal as 'minded to accept' (paragraph 11). Discussion about the case commenced at paragraph 17, from which point the judge consistently used the phrase 'minded to decide' when describing the July letters. That was not the correct way in which to refer to those letters, and it would appear that the evidence submitted on behalf of the Secretary of State must have been the source of the error.

According to the summary history, at the time decisions were taken in July, the Secretary of State was possessed of a report by independent financial consultants:

*To the effect that both of the proposals represented 'a medium risk' of not meeting the affordability criterion, but that both could be 'workable'* (para. 10).

That was an odd way in which to summarise the comparative perform-ance of the one and two unitary proposals on the Affordability criterion. As we have seen in Chapter 3, in July the DCLG was concerned that Bedford's proposal might not be Affordable because of the diseconomies of scale involved. Although the proposal was formally passed on this criterion, the Department wanted more work to be done on the financial case. That position contrasted markedly with the view taken of the county's single unitary proposal:

> *The Secretary of State considers that the financial case looks reasonably robust, although the projected savings figures appear very high and there is a risk that they could only be achieved if service levels were cut. Even if projected savings were un-realisable, however, there is a reasonable likelihood that the proposal would be likely to be affordable and could be funded.* (July letter to Bedfordshire CC.)

Both proposals were subject to risk, but the nature of the risk differed. For Bedford, the risk was thought to be that the proposal would not be Affordable. For the county, the risk was that the annual savings would be less than estimated but that nevertheless the proposal was Affordable. It would seem that, in relying on the Secretary of State's skeleton argument, the judge accepted seriously misleading information.

Much the most important concern about the Bedfordshire judgment is the following. Throughout the discussion part, Sir Robin Auld con-veyed the impression that, because the 2007 Act had conferred retro-spective authority for the Secretary of State to issue invitations and to undertake consultations, it was in fact perfectly proper for such action to be taken in anticipation. The Court of Appeal judgment was cited in a manner suggesting that the three judges concurred with the opinion of Underhill J in the High Court hearing of the Shrewsbury and Congleton case. At no point did the Bedfordshire judgment recognise the anxieties expressed by the Appeal Court about the use of non-statutory processes in a situation where there is statutory provision for how things should be done.

The fact that the Bedfordshire judgment failed to acknowledge the impropriety of acting in anticipation of legislation in a situation where there is relevant legislative provision is troubling. We have already noted the willingness of the Government to misinterpret the Court of Appeal's judgment (see the conclusion to Chapter 6) and the worry must be that, in the, future Ministers will again be tempted to act unlawfully ahead of pending legislation.

# 8

# Impact of the 2006-2008 LGR, origins and explanation

By April 2008, the parliamentary process had been completed to abolish seven county councils and create nine unitary authorities – five as county unitaries and two counties both to be divided into two councils. Vesting day will be 1 April 2009 for all the new councils. In addition, there is unfinished business in Devon, Norfolk and Suffolk as the Boundary Committee ponders the advice it will offer to the Secretary of State about unitary structures in those counties. Table 8.1 summarises the map of England as now determined, taking no account of possible changes in the three outstanding county areas.

The fact that there are still three counties whose future remains to be decided means that there is an important element of uncertainty about the structure of local government in two tier areas. However, the uncertainties run deeper and wider than just those three counties.

## No hidden plans?

The Grand Committee of the House of Lords considered the five Orders for creating unitary counties at one sitting, treating the business in some respects like a second reading debate on a Bill. During the proceedings, Baroness Andrews, speaking for the Government, revealed the ambivalent attitudes of Ministers, as shown by the following:

*I assure the noble Lord* [Baroness Hollis] *that <u>we do not have hidden plans for future change or a rolling programme up our sleeves.</u> During the debate on the local government Bill, I said several times that we have no plans for a rolling programme, restructuring or any further invitations to councils. As the Noble Baroness, Lady Scott, said, we are where we are now with other aspects of this initiative. We have some way to go with the outstanding councils and there is no rolling programme, but we recognise that in certain areas <u>there might in future be an appetite for more unitary structures and it might be right to issue a targeted and focused invitation, but under specific and exceptional circumstances.</u> This programme has been discrete and sufficient unto itself.* (Hansard 21 February 2008, col. GC 39.)

Stated thus, the LGR was treated as a discrete programme, 'sufficient unto itself'. However, later that same afternoon, when the discussion was focusing on the Order for Cornwall, a different impression was conveyed. Lord Teversham observed:

*The order is very much concerned with the future. Generally, in Cornwall we see this as a very important step, but it is only a first step towards <u>bringing other powers and responsibilities down to the Cornwall Council</u> once it has shown itself to be a responsible, effective and successful authority: powers relating to <u>the economy, social issues and perhaps even health issues</u> ... There will be an important duty ... to ensure that it fully devolves its own powers locally as much as possible.* (Hansard 21 February 2008, col. GC 57.)

Lord Teversham was reflecting the view that was widespread in Cornwall during the LGR, that a unitary county could acquire responsibilities currently exercised at the regional level or by other bodies, such health trusts.

The response from Baroness Andrews about the LGR in general was revealing:

*I am very happy to repeat what my right honourable friend said in the other place. <u>This is very much the leading edge of our devolution proposals: it has not been a series of one-off considerations, but part of a movement to demonstrate that we really do want to take the next step and the one after, from devolution to double-devolution,</u> not least in terms of neighbourhoods and local areas.* (Hansard 21 February 2008, col. GC 57.)

The Government would have one simultaneously believe: that the LGR was a one-off event, sufficient unto itself; and that it was the leading edge of devolution proposals. This stretches credulity to an impossible degree. The Government might respond that the LGR and the Pathfinder programme should be regarded as an experiment. At the time invitations for both kinds of proposal were issued in 2006, it was made clear that new unitary councils would be subjected to independent long term evaluation, including performance with respect to the 'previous two-tier arrangements' (DCLG 2006b, para. 5.23). Were this explanation to be offered, the rejoinder would be that there are other ways to assess the relative performance of different structures of local government, and that

### Table 8.1
Size of local authorities
Population 2006
000

|  | Average | Smallest | Largest |
|---|---|---|---|
| 9 new unitaries | 348 | Bedford 153 | Cornwall 524 |
| 46 existing unitaries | 182 | Rutland 37 | Bristol 394 |
| 36 Metropolitan councils | 304 | S. Tyneside 145 | Birmingham 992 |
| 32 London boroughs | 236 | Kingston 152 | Croydon 341 |
| 27 remaining counties | 756 | Dorset 405 | Kent 1,371 |
| 207 constituent districts | 99 | Teesdale 25 | Northampton 200 |

Source: CIPFA 2006.

the Government has issued no such evaluation. In any case, there is the sense among many in local government that if, or when, a further opportunity arises to make unitary proposals, there will be numerous bids submitted, by councils disappointed in 2006-2008 and by others. This sense is itself destabilising, and a hindrance to improvement.

Baroness Andrews has signalled the possibility that there might in future be an 'appetite' for more unitary structures, hedging the proposition with caveats that imply limited change in special circumstances, suggesting that there may be further piecemeal change. Therefore, two matters deserve urgent attention. First, does the structure of local government as it will be from 2009 appear to be sensible, and if not why? Second, does the 2007 Act make adequate provision for the future consideration of structural matters in England?

## A curious patchwork

Crude though it may be, total population provides the single most useful measure by which to consider the structure of local authorities, and the relevant data are shown in Table 8.1. On average, the nine new unitary councils are nearly twice the size of the 46 unitary authorities that were created in the LGR conducted in the 1990s, and 50% larger than the average London borough. Bedford, the smallest of the new unitary councils, is four times larger than Rutland, the smallest of the unitaries created somewhat over a decade ago. At the other end of the scale, Cornwall, with somewhat over 0.5 million people, is bigger than any of the existing unitary councils, bigger than all the London boroughs, and only exceeded by Birmingham and Leeds among the Metropolitan councils. So what may this tell us about the suitability of the smaller London and Metropolitan councils, and many of the existing unitary councils?

Consider these facts in association with two matters. First, when the Government planned to have elected regional assemblies, the Boundary Committee was asked to propose two possible unitary structures for each of the counties in northern England. In every case, the options put before the electorate were a unitary county or, depending on the county, two or three councils for the county area. Those proposals reflected a substantial change in thinking about the appropriate size of councils from what was in vogue in the 1990s. Second, the July 2007 letters of the recent LGR made it clear that the Government was concerned that unitary councils below the size of a whole county would lose economies of scale, although, perversely, two counties were divided and Bedford was regarded as acceptable as a unitary council. Notwithstanding the Government's ambivalence, the direction, of change appears to be towards substantially larger local authorities, and this must call in question structures across England. Indeed, Mr Ken Livingstone has made it clear that he thinks the number of London boroughs should be reduced from 32 to just five.

These pressures point to the need to consider the structure of local government not just in the remaining two tier areas but for England as a whole, with a view to enlargement. However, it is predictable that there will be pressure in the opposite direction, particularly where there are large unitary councils, such as the new councils for county areas. The proposals for area governance within the county unitaries and for the two Cheshire councils are so limited that they will not provide the local 'empowerment' proclaimed by Ministers. This situation may result in the build-up of pressure to re-invent significant elements of two tier arrangements, and it is uncertain where such pressure might lead. Consequently, there is the prospect of this additional source of instability for the future. In any case, it is not so long ago that a version of two tier arrangements was brought back for London, and the Government has indicated that it is thinking about similar arrangements for the former Metropolitan county areas. Some serious thought needs to be given to these conflicting pressures – how can one balance the need for genuine local empowerment with the apparent need for larger scale administration?

The LGR has contributed to the curious patchwork of local government in England and the outstanding business with the Boundary Committee illustrates the de-stabilising effect that it has had. The Committee has been asked to consider Exeter, Ipswich and Norwich, cities whose boundaries are tightly drawn. The Boundary Committee will need to consider whether to recommend boundary extensions for these cities and how any such change would impact on the rest of the county, focussing on the options that there may be for creating viable county-wide unitary structures. In Devon, there is the related task of considering the boundaries of the two existing unitary councils, Plymouth and Torbay. Whatever happens, the final outcomes will have implications across England. If, as is possible, cities are enlarged and new unitary councils created for Exeter, Ipswich and Norwich, with new unitary structures for the three counties, then important precedents will have been set for other cities, such as Derby, Leicester and Nottingham. The fact that county boundaries are no longer sacrosanct adds to the potential for instability.

Any reorganisation involves questions about the appropriate names for local authorities and the associated matter of personal identification with a defined territorial entity. This was a major issue in 1974, one that recurred in the 1990s and has surfaced again with the LGR. One example will suffice to illustrate the problem. Bedfordshire is to be divided into two unitary councils; one, Bedford, will be a non-metropolitan county, while the other authority will be known as Central Bedfordshire, but central to what? Members of the public could be forgiven if they find themselves confused as to where they belong.

Beyond reasonable doubt, the LGR has de-stabilised the structure of local government in shire England and, indeed, in the main urban areas. This has reinforced the need to consider the purpose and financing of local government. Unfortunately, the 2007 Act does not provide an appropriate framework for this kind of wider consideration. Instead, it allows further piecemeal change to take place, with the implication that the structure of local government may become even less easily justified than is currently the case.

### Future re-organisation procedures: the 2007 Act

Under the Local Government and Public Involvement in Health Act 2007, the Secretary of State may invite any principal authority to submit proposals to him for structural re-organisation. Upon receipt of the proposals, he may decide to take no action. However, if he wishes to take action, he may ask the Boundary Committee for advice before any Order would be laid before Parliament, or he could proceed directly to consultation and then implementation by Order (Sections 4(2) and 7(1)). There is no certainty that the Boundary Committee would be involved, leaving the way open for the Secretary of State to proceed in exactly the same manner as was the case with the 2006-2008 LGR. This is a major departure from prior practice; under the 1992 Act, it was for the Boundary Committee, upon receipt of a direction to examine a given area, to formulate proposals and to make recommendations.

If the Boundary Committee were to be asked for advice on a proposal, it could recommend either acceptance or rejection thereof, or could recommend an alternative scheme. Recommendations received by the Secretary of State could be rejected, or accepted, with or without modifications. The building blocks for proposals to be made to the Secretary of State, and possibly referred to the Boundary committee, are whole existing local authorities, and it is clear that new unitary councils could be created that straddle existing county boundaries, as may be recommended by the Boundary Committee in their consideration of Norfolk and Suffolk. They might recommend the union of Great Yarmouth and Lowestoft.

The 1992 Act had some provisions that have been omitted from the 2007 Act. Previously, when the Secretary of State directed the Boundary Committee to review an area, the Committee had to consider the 'identities and interests of local communities' and also the need for 'effective and convenient local government'. These requirements are no longer enshrined in statute for the consideration of local government structures, nor are there any equivalent stipulations. Therefore, the terms on which the Boundary Committee will operate depend much more upon the 'guidance' that will be issued by the Secretary of State, and the criteria that he chooses to set. Consequently, the independence of the Committee may be less than hitherto, and the power of the Secretary of State may be greater.

The 2007 Act has watered down the statutory protections in another way. Under the 1992 Act, the Boundary Committee was expressly enjoined to consult 'those who may have an interest' in proposals, a formulation which covered members of the public as well as other bodies. The new statutory regime contains no provision regarding who should be consulted by a principal authority when unitary proposals are being prepared, the matter presumably being covered in the guidance that would be issued by the Secretary of State. Furthermore, if he has received a proposal from a principal authority and wishes to implement it, then he must consult on the proposal before laying an Order. This consultation must include the affected local authorities and 'such other persons as he considers appropriate' (Section 7(3)(b)). On the experience of the recent LGR, 'appropriate' persons would be stakeholders and partners, but not members of the public.

These provisions are at odds with the requirement on the Boundary Committee if it wishes to propose a scheme alternative to one remitted by the Secretary of State. For this purpose, the Committee must 'take such steps as they consider sufficient to secure that persons who may be interested' are informed of the proposals (Section 9(3)(b)), and all representations must be taken into account in assessing the proposal. This provision clearly means that the public must be suitably informed, because every citizen in an affected area could be expected to be potentially 'interested'. It is difficult to imagine that the Committee would decline to take seriously the results of polls and referenda that might be submitted as part of the consultation process.

The Act sets out consultation rules that differ according to the proposal being considered – the original proposal submitted by a principal authority, or an alternative scheme being considered by the Boundary Committee. That is unacceptably sloppy legislation, leaving the Secretary of State with fewer constraints on his procedure than have been placed on the Boundary Committee.

At this stage, let us summarise the changes that the 2007 Act has introduced by comparison with the 1992 Act. Three statutory principles have been discarded:

- The requirement that proposals must be provide for effective and convenient local government.

- The need to reflect the identities and interests of local communities.

- With the exception noted above, the concept of members of the public being 'persons who may be interested' in proposals.

When the Bill was published that became the 2007 Act, it stipulated that the Secretary of State could direct a local authority to prepare a unitary proposal, a power that was retained in the Act except that it explicitly lapsed on 25 January 2008. No direction was given, but had one been issued this could only have been done in the circumstance that:

> *The Secretary of State believes that giving the direction would be in the interests of* <u>*effective and convenient local government*</u> (2007 Act, Section 3(1)(b)).

There was then, and is now, no obligation on the Secretary of State to consider whether a proposal received in response to an invitation fulfils the 'effective and convenient local government' requirement. This can only be described as perverse.

### Summary

For our purpose, there are two key features of the 2007 Act. First, there is no requirement that the Boundary Committee would be asked to make recommendations. The Secretary of State has the power to proceed in exactly the same way as was adopted for the 2006-2008 LGR, with the potential that all the faults we have identified with that process could be repeated. Second, important statutory safeguards that existed in the 1992 Act have been dropped – the requirement for convenient and effective local government, identities and interests of local communities and the near elimination of public opinion as a factor to be considered. The effect is to give the Secretary of State considerably more power than was formerly the case. One has to ask whether the legislation was drafted for the convenience of Ministers, rather than as a statement of the openness and accountability in the democratic process that is necessary for gaining the assent of the governed?

## An LGR at odds with other policies

The LGR and the way it was conducted contradicted important aspects of the Government's declared intentions in a broad sweep of policies across many sectors of the economy. However, to keep the discussion within bounds, we will explore the contradictions by comparing some features of the White Paper, *Strong and Prosperous Communities* (DCLG 2006a), with the LGR that it initiated, focusing in particular on two matters of central importance – efficiency, and citizen/neighbourhood empowerment.

### *Efficiency*

The White Paper stated that the creation of unitary councils would improve efficiency, and that where two tier arrangements remain it would be essential for those councils 'to achieve similar levels of improvement and efficiency gains to those we are expecting of the new unitaries' (paras 3.55 and 3.59). The point was underlined later in the document as a general requirement for all local authorities to achieve 'ambitious efficiency gains' as part of the 2007 Comprehensive Spending Review (para. 7.10). The rhetoric cannot be faulted.

However, as we have noted in Chapter 1, Members of Parliament have found themselves unable to accept claims made by central government departments regarding their own annual Gershon efficiency savings, identifying eight ways in which the figures have been fudged. The equivalent problem with the LGR has been the willingness of the DCLG to accept dodgy financial data in the business cases compiled to support unitary bids. If the Government wishes to be taken seriously about the need for greater efficiency, then it must take steps to ensure that, in future, much more rigorous standards are applied to the appraisal of policy initiatives than were applied during the LGR, a lesson that apparently has not been learned from the LGR conducted in the 1990s (see Chisholm 2000a).

### The public

The introduction to the White Paper was written by Ruth Kelly, as the Secretary of State. She said:

> *Local government's strength is its closeness to its communities. <u>Citizens and communities</u> know what they want from public services, and what needs to be done to improve the places where they live. We want to use these strengths to drive up service standards and foster a sense of community and civic pride.*

The executive summary reinforced the point with the following:

> *This White Paper is on the side of <u>individuals and families</u> who want to make a difference, both to their own lives and to the communities in which they live.*

Some strands of recent policy have been consistent with these declarations, for example, the 2004 referendum in the northeast on whether to have a regional elected assembly, and the requirement to hold a local poll on the introduction of elected mayors. Elected regional assemblies were abandoned after the negative northeast vote, marking, one might say, a victory for people power. On the other hand, the Government has decided that it is too difficult to get the requisite majority for elected mayors; the 2007 Act scrapped the need for local referenda, making it easier to effect the change irrespective of public opinion.

On 27 December 2007, Secretary of State Hazel Blears issued a press release under the heading 'Petition power kicks off new year of community action' (see Jones and Stewart 2008). The proposal publicised for consultation was for local authorities to have a legal duty to 'respond to any petition gaining sufficient local support' – the suggested threshold being 250 signatures. Included in the press release was a note for editors:

> *The petition powers duty follows the recently signed concordat which makes clear that 'both local and central government have the responsibility to devolve power and engage and empower <u>communities and individual citizens</u> – in debate and decision making and in shaping and delivering services'.*

Compare this press release with the Sustainable Communities Act 2007:

*In this Act references to promoting the sustainability of local communities, in relation to a local authority, are references to encouraging the improvement of the economic, social or environmental well-being of the authority's area, or part of its area ... In this section 'social well-being' <u>includes participation in civic and political activity</u>. (Sections 1(2) and 1(3).)*

It is impossible to reconcile these declarations about involving citizens with the attitude taken by the DCLG during the LGR, that public opinion was not important and could be ignored. Nor are the declarations consistent with the provisions of the 2007 Act for future consideration of structural change in two tier areas, provisions that have reduced the role of citizens in the consultation process. Action speaks louder than words, and the action shows that the Government apparently has no intention of granting real power to people, and is actually taking it away. The rhetoric does not match the reality.

### Councillors

Local councillors are said to be the 'bedrock of local democracy' (DCLG 2006a, para. 3.10). If the White Paper is to be believed, councillors are to have enhanced roles, as champions for their communities and simultaneously providing greater strategic leadership. They are to supposed to have new powers to match the expanded duties, and should benefit from 'capacity building' to provide them with support.

These intentions do not sit easily with the creation of unitary councils covering large areas and with populations exceeding most existing councils. The total number of councillors in unitary counties will be reduced by 50%, even 75%. It is very difficult to see how they will have the time and resources to take on more duties while simultaneously having, on average, much larger electorates to represent. Some of the July letters acknowledged that there may be a problem of 'remoteness', but the issue was not properly addressed. In the extreme case, Cornwall, the Government indulged in what can only be described as wishful thinking when it was suggested that the existing number of county councillors might be doubled. In any case, the Government was willing to accept 'top down' area governance in Co. Durham, and arrangements in Bedfordshire that involved 'little real delegation', directly belying the rhetoric.

The ambivalence of the Government is emphasised by some comments in the White Paper about district councils in two tier areas:

*District councils have an essential role in place-shaping. They lead on many of the services which are essential to delivering the strategic priorities in the county-wide LAA [Local Area Agreement], including housing, planning and some leisure services. They are also essential for building strong links with local people, neighbourhoods and parish councils.* (DCLG 2006a, para. 5.52.)

The fundamental problem is that proper area governance in unitary counties would cost considerably more than has been budgeted, significantly reducing the net saving that would be possible. Again, action seems to speak louder than words.

### Rhetoric and reality

These few examples, all directly related to the LGR and its White Paper progenitor, raise a troubling question. Do Ministers believe their own rhetoric? If we assume that they do, then perhaps two explanations may be offered. It may be that central government has become impossibly complex and compartmentalised, so that genuinely joined up thinking has become exceedingly difficult, even impossible. Alternatively, and consistent with the LGR experience, the slippery use of language permits the reconciliation of the irreconcilable, the extreme case of which that we have reported being the re-definition of 'broad cross section of support' to whether a new unitary authority 'will work for local people' (p. 24). When language is used in this way, virtually anything can be treated as being consistent with anything else.

## The a-historical approach to the LGR

In Chapter 1, we briefly alluded to the re-organisations of local government that occurred in 1974 and during the 1990s. It is now appropriate to expand on that account, and to consider whether the 2006-2008 LGR shows that lessons from recent history had been heeded. This enquiry has implications for any future proposals to change the structure of local government.

At the close of the Second World War in 1945, England and Wales had a mosaic of small authorities with differing powers. There were county councils and county boroughs, municipal and London boroughs, and urban and rural districts. Excluding the London boroughs, there were 1,502 local councils above the network of parish councils (Chisholm 1975, p. 306). Outside London, and with the exception of the county boroughs, this was a complex two tier arrangement which, with the return of peace, came to be seen as not fit for purpose on account of the multiplicity of small councils with differing powers.

The first change was the creation of the Greater London Council in 1965, a two tier arrangement for the metropolis. During the 1960s, thoughts also turned to what should be done elsewhere in England and Wales, and also in Scotland, where there were similar problems. The Redcliffe-Maud Royal Commission (1969) majority report recommended 58 unitary councils covering the whole of England other than London and three Metropolitan regions. The Greater London Council would continue, and for three conurbations there would be county councils and a total of 20 districts. A powerful dissenting report was written by Mr Derek Senior, advocating 35 regions in England outside London, four of which would be all-purpose councils, the remaining ones having a total of 143 second tier councils.

The Labour government broadly accepted the majority proposals but lost power in the 1970 general election, and the incoming Conservative administration obtained the Local Government Act 1972 that created the two tier arrangements which have survived to the present day. Although the new Government did not set up its own commission to examine the structure of local government, it had the benefit of the Royal Commission's work and Senior's minority report, plus the widespread and vocal reactions thereto.

Parliament defined the county boundaries, and also two tier arrangements for the Metropolitan (conurbation) areas. The Local Government Boundary Commission was asked to recommend the structure of districts within the shire counties, having been given clear and reasonably precise guidelines for the purpose. Their recommendations were accepted, without modification.

Implemented in 1974, the change in England and Wales was radical. Excluding London, the number of councils had been reduced from 1,502 to 422, virtually all of this reduction accounted for by the smaller number of second tier councils. The two tier structure of local government had been re-modelled, and the whole of England was administered by variants of this arrangement. That such a dramatic change was possible with very little dissent reflected the fact that there was a problem to be solved, there was general agreement that something had to be done, and a workable solution had been devised. An important feature of the re-organisation was the joint consideration of powers and structure, reflecting a view of what local government was supposed to do. However, questions of finance were not addressed.

The seeds of future trouble had been sown. The county boroughs had been demoted, now having the same status as the other districts in shire England. This offended civic pride on the one hand, and political sensitivities on the other, because these cities were traditional Labour strongholds. The other problem was the existence of the Greater London Council and the Metropolitan counties, powerful political bodies, controlled by Labour and hostile to a subsequent Conservative government. The simple solution was to abolish those awkward elected upper tiers – the Greater London Council and the Metropolitan counties – transferring their powers to lower tier authorities. This politically motivated change occurred in 1986, followed by the abolition of the Inner London Education Authority in 1990. In practice, the two tier structures had not been abolished but had been transformed into complex webs of unelected joint committees and other versions of joint arrangements (Leach *et al.* 1991).

Labour held power for a period in the 1970s, during which time they sought to deal with the large cities, publishing a White Paper entitled *Organic Change in Local Government* (DOE 1979), but nothing came of this initiative with the return of the Conservatives to office. Nothing was done in shire England until the fiasco with the Poll Tax. To mask the retreat from this unpopular impost, and its replacement with the Council Tax, Mr Michael Heseltine initiated what purported to be a thorough review of local government, including funding. In practice, the Council Tax initiative was separate from structural re-organisation, and there was no consideration given to the powers of local authorities beyond the idea of combining district and county responsibilities by creating unitary authorities.

At the time the Local Government Act 1992 was passed, there was an idea circulating in academia, 'public choice theory', arguing the benefits of small all-purpose local authorities as a way of providing 'choice' for citizens and driving up the quality of service delivery. However, lacking the courage of its convictions in England, the Government was unwilling to legislate for major change (in contrast to Scotland and Wales). Instead, the Act set up the Local Government Commission for England, charged to examine the whole of shire England and to make recommendations for structural change or no change. The Act was badly drafted, the guidance given to the Commission was muddled and the in-fighting between authorities was bitter. The Commission took pains to find out what members of the public thought about proposals, showing that, in the majority of cases, citizens were not persuaded that change was needed. In the event, three counties, newly created in 1974, were abolished and 46 unitary councils were established, including the big cities that had been restive since 1974 (Chisholm 2000b, 2002).

Although the Government wanted unitary solutions, the 1992 Act and the guidance given to the Commission were contradictory and imprecise. There was no 'blueprint'. In other words, on this occasion there was a solution in search of a problem.

One lesson to be learned from the 1990s is that a long drawn-out review process is not a good idea. It would seem that the Government had learned this lesson when the LGR was announced in October 2006, because the intention was that final decisions would be announced in July 2007. In the event, the ostensibly final decisions were not announced until December at the earliest. For those authorities under review, the process was no quicker in 2006-2008 than in the 1990s.

However, focusing on the desirability of having a quick process seems to have obscured the more important questions. As in the 1990s, the Government offered no blueprint for the structure of local government, beyond the belief that unitary councils are better than two tier authorities. But that belief is belied by the facts that the Greater London Authority was established in 2000, at the same time as the post of elected mayor was created, and that the Government has been pondering similar changes for the Metropolitan areas of England. Two tier arrangements are said to be bad for shire England, but are, apparently, good for conurbations.

Several lessons can be learned from the experience of the Local Government Commission for England in the 1990s. First, estimates of the costs and benefits of structural change were erroneous – transition costs were substantially under-estimated and recurrent savings were exaggerated. Second, the claim that two tiers create confusion proved difficult to verify, because all local authorities interact with a multitude of other agencies, statutory and non-statutory. If individuals are confused as to whether the county or district is responsible for something, those confusions did not loom large by comparison with uncertainties regarding responsibility for many services, a problem that has been increased by the growth of the contract economy. Third, the argument that unitary structures would streamline management and service delivery ignores an important trade-off. If there is a small number of large councils, there will be fewer external relations than if there are many small councils. On the other hand, moving from a large number of councils to a smaller number increases the need for internal mechanisms to be in place, so that the interests and aspirations of the various areas may be recognised and heeded. It is often said that two tier arrangements cause conflict, but this overlooks the fact that these structures articulate the interests which differ geographically. Re-arranging boundaries does not alter the underlying geography and itself does nothing to ensure that minority interests can be heard.

Although the Government did not issue a set of guidelines regarding the size of possible new unitary councils for the 2006-2008 LGR the dominant thinking appears to have been that larger councils are more likely to be efficient while providing an adequate level of internal devolution. For this reason, unitary counties were to be preferred to unitary districts. This is in marked contrast to the 1990s, when the political pressure was in favour of unitary districts. The fact that conventional wisdom can change so markedly in so short a period of time indicates that there is no settled view of a 'problem' to be solved, comparable to the consensus that existed in the 1960s/early 1970s.

During the last few decades, local government has been subjected to enormous changes, most of which have been piecemeal - alteration of the powers exercised by councils, duties laid upon them and alterations to the funding regime. Structural change ought to be considered in this wider context, on the basis of what local government is for (Lyons 2007), on the old principle of form following function. That fundamental lesson had not been learned when the 2006-2008 LGR was launched.

> If men could learn from history,
> what lessons it might teach us!
> But passion and party blind our eyes,
> and the light which experience gives us
> is a lantern on the stern,
> which shines only on the waves behind us!
>
> (Samuel Taylor Coleridge, *Youth and Age*)

## Some speculations

Why, one may ask, did the Government embark on the LGR? After all, as late as March 2006, the Local Government Minister, Mr Woolas, gave an apparently categorical assurance that the Government did not intend forcing re-structuring upon reluctant councils:

> *Restructuring without local agreement is 99.999% ruled out. I'm not aware of anywhere that's likely (Local Government Chronicle* 9 March 2006, p. 1).

Although less categorical, the 2006 invitation to councils to submit proposals echoed the sentiment, indicating that proposals would only come forward where there was strong support for change. Nevertheless, re-organisation is proceeding despite the lack of local agreement.

Three possible reasons for undertaking the LGR may be ruled out. First, there was no widely accepted 'problem' comparable to that which existed in the 1970s, creating the need for structural change. Second, there was no political conflict between central and local government of the kind that contributed to the demise of the Greater London Council and the Metropolitan counties. Third, there was no crisis comparable to the Poll Tax fiasco requiring cover for an embarrassing political retreat. Consequently, one must look elsewhere for reasons.

After the May 2005 general election, Mr David Miliband became Secretary of State for the newly created DCLG and quickly developed a distinctive agenda focussed on neighbourhood empowerment. He spent a considerable amount of time meeting local authority representatives around England, and the question of re-structuring was an issue at those meetings. It would seem that those discussions provided the initial impetus. It is understood that Mr Miliband was involved in drafting the White Paper that had been promised for 2006 but he moved to another office following a ministerial reshuffle in May of that year. Consequently, part way through the task, he was replaced by Ruth Kelly. She lacked local government experience and we may surmise that civil servants took control over the White Paper and associated policy developments.

That surmise is consistent with the following. Shortly before the White Paper was published, one local authority chief executive reported to us a conversation with a senior DCLG civil servant. During this conversation, the DCLG officer extolled the administrative benefit to the Department of dealing with unitary councils instead with counties and districts in two tier areas. On the assumption that unitary councils would be compliant, there probably would be administrative advantages. If that were the motivation, then the policy could be packaged as part of the general efficiency drive of the Government on the one hand, and of steps towards neighbourhood and community empowerment on the other. Once the ball had been set rolling, it would have been difficult indeed to stop it.

## Conclusion

The 2006-2007 LGR has amounted to piecemeal tinkering with the structure of local government, but tinkering with substantial de-stabilising implications. As matters currently stand, the 2007 Act will enable further piecemeal changes to be made by the Secretary of State, subject only to the need to obtain the passage of an Order through Parliament. He would be able to act in the manner that we have de-scribed and documented, a manner that has paid scant regard to evidence and consistency, and has largely ignored the wishes of citizens. Local government, it would seem, has been taken for a ride, something that reminds one of the lady of Riga:

> There was a young lady of Riga,
> Who rode with a smile on a tiger;
> They returned from the ride,
> With the lady inside,
> And the smile on the face of the tiger.
>
> (Langford Reed *The Limerick Book*)

# 9

# Taking liberties

*Where information is not available to the Government, or otherwise, the*
*Government may when considering a proposal make such assumptions*
*and estimates as it sees fit* (DCLG 2006b, para. 5.6).

The words quoted above are taken from the 2006 invitation to councils
to submit unitary proposals. They are contained in the text about Stage 1
of the process after proposals had been submitted in January 2007, the
stage leading up to the decisions announced in March that sixteen
proposals would go forward for consultation. It is extraordinary that the
Government should have chosen the words 'as it sees fit', instead of
using a phrase like 'as it judges to be reasonable'. In the clearest possible
terms, the Government was claiming the privilege to make whatever
assumptions and estimates it wanted to, without regard to any test of
plausibility or reasonableness. That claim severs the roots of civilised
discourse, and hence the foundations of an elective democracy.

It is no defence for the Government to say that the provision in paragraph 5.6 applied only to Stage 1, where information might be lacking,
and probably was. Whatever the deficiencies, the assumptions and
estimates that may have been necessary should have been subject to the
test of reasonableness. In any case, with but limited exceptions in the
case of the unitary proposals that went forward for implementation, the
financial figures submitted by local authorities in January 2007 were
hardly changed at the end of the consultation period in June, which
carries with it the implication that any assumptions and estimates based
on the 'as it sees fit' claim were, once made, adhered to throughout the
review process, which in turn implies that the DCLG 'saw fit' to dismiss
criticisms without actually responding thereto.

From the beginning, the DCLG had shown its hand, declaring that it would be the sole judge and would act without the normal constraint of trying to be reasonable. The same message was conveyed at the end of the process, in the debate on the Order to implement a unitary Wiltshire. Mr Healey, Minister for Local Government, used the following words during the debate in the House of Commons:

> *The extent and the nature of the <u>evidence</u> that any proposing authority submit-ted in order to meet those tests* [the five criteria] *clearly <u>varied</u>. Some failed; others that passed would have gone about their task by meeting those five tests and demonstrating that they could meet them in different ways, and they did so. ... With the exception of some of the financial analysis that we did, where it was possible to subject numbers to a test, a matter of judgment was inevita-bly involved. ... We made that judgment <u>on the back of consistent evidence,</u> clearly set out in published criteria ...* (Hansard 5 February 2008, col. 910.)

There was a grave lack of logic in these words. Varied information was portrayed as providing consistent evidence, a proposition that is impossi-ble to accept. There was no evidence set out in the criteria, and those criteria were not clear. Nevertheless, the Minister wanted to convey the impression that, because the same five criteria had been used, the decision process had been consistent. The minister was in fact articulat-ing the Humpty Dumpty doctrine (p. **52**), which effectively says that there is no common meaning to language. Mr Healey's approach to his parliamentary colleagues exactly matched the contradictory and inconsis-tent approach of the DCLG to the whole exercise; he was conforming with the self-serving rule enunciated in October 2006 that introduces the present chapter.

There was a further irony in Mr Healey's statement to Parliament. He said that it was possible to subject numbers in the Wiltshire financial case 'to a test', although he did not elaborate on the nature of the test applied. Implicit in his comments was the idea that financial detail could be examined 'objectively', independently of any judgements, an implication that is nonsensical. Unitary proposals were supported by financial appraisals the coverage of which varied from one case to another in a manner that cannot be explained by differing local circumstances. Significant cost and saving items were estimated in ways that were questionable, and in some cases fallacious. In Wiltshire, for example, the on-going cost of the devolved governance proposed by the county, at

£0.9 million p.a., could not provide much local empowerment. Mr Healey's statement that there was consistent evidence did not accord with the truth.

### How fared the four criteria we proposed in Chapter 1?

Four general criteria were suggested in Chapter 1 by which to judge the LGR process. Regrettably, not one was met. As we have seen, the rules changed as the LGR progressed, especially with regard to the interpretation of the five criteria – the shift from hurdles to be surmounted before decisions were taken to the 'reasonable likelihood' of fulfilment after a new council had been established. Although 'service users/citizens' were recognised as having an interest, public opinion was discounted or ignored where citizens were opposed to proposals. A mockery was made of the 'legitimate expectation' of those involved.

The rules also changed for financial assessments. Initially, it seemed clear that there would be shadow authorities, for which provision should be made in assessing transition costs, but in practice many of the new councils will be continuing authorities. Rules were also changed for the annual grant to councils for the 'cost of being business'. It was expected early on that, where there would be fewer councils on account of amalgamation, annual grants would be lost for every authority abolished, but part way through the process it was announced that the grants would continue for at least three years.

Inconsistency was the hallmark of the way in which the evidence was evaluated and the five criteria applied. The DCLG decision letters reveal inconsistencies on major matters, a selective use of evidence, misleading presentations of evidence and reliance on financial estimates that contained obvious deficiencies. This inconsistency reflected, at least in part, the absence of clear goals. According to the Government, the LGR was a one-off 'window of opportunity' to create unitary councils, with no plans for a continuing programme of structural change. On the other hand, the new unitary councils were supposed to be at the 'leading edge' of improvements in local government. Confusion at this level was matched by confusion over the detail, in that the Government recognised the probability that scale economies would be lost if county councils were broken up but was willing to accept financial estimates for sub-county unitaries inconsistent with that expectation. Because there was no blueprint for the future, those involved in the process did not know where they stood.

Inconsistency with other Government policies also marked the LGR, most particularly the contrast between the rhetoric of involving citizens and the reality that citizens' voices were not heeded if the message was antagonistic to proposals. Effective consultation and involvement cannot be built on the basis that only the 'right' opinions, as judged by the Government, will be heeded.

Because of these and other shortcomings, the decisions reached by the Government were not backed by clear and consistent judgements. The decision letters reveal muddled and contradictory thinking, comparing one decision with another, and even within decision letters. Therefore, taking account of these deficiencies, the analysis we have presented confirms what we said in Chapter 1, the procedures adopted by the DCLG fell a long way short of the standards to be expected if business is to be conducted properly.

## Taking liberties with Parliament

Nominated for a 2008 BAFTA award, the film 'Taking Liberties' is a searing indictment of the way in which civil liberties have been and are being eroded in Britain. The film does not deal directly with the relationship between the Government and Parliament, or the Executive and the Legislature, but this issue is crucial if a free democracy is to survive. Over the years, Parliament has become increasingly like a poodle to the Government, instead of being the bastion of freedom against an overweening administration, and the 2006-08 LGR both exemplified this fact and reinforced the trend.

When the LGR was initiated in 2006, there was statutory provision for the way in which the structure of local government could be altered, involving a reference to the Boundary Committee and recommendations from that body, which the Secretary of State could accept or reject, or make minor changes. The Government chose to ignore this procedure, inventing an entirely new one that gave the Secretary of State complete control over the process and decision making, thereby breaking a long tradition that it is either Parliament that decides these matters directly through primary legislation, or by means of Orders placed by the Secretary of State after a process involving the independent Boundary Committee or its predecessors. This novel process was initiated before the Local Government and Public Involvement in Health Bill had even been published, which Bill contained provisions, carried forward into the Act, to give retrospective authority for actions being taken.

Two of the Appeal Court judges in the Shrewsbury and Congleton judicial review expressed their grave reservations about the 'wholly non-statutory procedure' used by the DCLG. As Carnwath LJ said, 'it seems to me a constitutional principle of some importance that local authorities should be able to rely on the safeguards of a statutory process'. The Government took liberties with those safeguards. In so doing, they took liberties with Parliament, whose legislation was flouted.

Somewhat over a decade ago, the House of Lords Select Committee on Relations between Central and Local Government concentrated on the 'present realities within the existing constitutional settlement' (1996, para. 3.1). Acting as it did with the LGR, the Government ruptured that constitutional settlement. Is the rupture to be repaired and, if so, how may this done? Our concern is that something must be done, lest:

> *The traditional institution of local government … become increasingly demoralised, and even fade away into nothing, its passing unmourned by many who might later regret its absence* (SCRCLG 1996, para. 1.1).

The context in which these wider issues ought to be considered has changed markedly in recent years, with the talk that there might be a 'constitution' for the National Health Service, and the Prime Minister floating the idea that there might be a national written constitution.

Another cause for concern is the following. Once the Bill had been tabled which became the Local Government and Public Involvement in Health Act 2007, there could be no absolute certainty that the retrospective provisions would survive to reach the statute book, yet the Government acted on the assumption that they would. In other words, Parliament was taken for granted. This assumption was a realistic assessment of the political realities. However, to assume that retrospective powers would be enacted was taking liberties with Parliament as an institution.

In any case, the Bill might have failed entirely had a General Election been called in the autumn of 2007, as at one time seemed probable. If Parliament had been dissolved, there would have been political horse-trading about which legislation would be enacted – Bills in their entirety would have been at risk of lapsing, or of being truncated. There is no way of knowing whether the 2007 Act would have survived, or whether, if it had, the retrospective provisions would have been removed. If, for any reason, the Local Government and Public Involvement in Health Bill had not been enacted, or had lost the retrospective provisions, then a substantial number of local authorities, other public bodies and private citizens would have been put through an exercise using valuable financial and other resources to no purpose, and with no basis for claiming recompense.

Why did the Government decide to initiate and then follow through on the LGR before there was legislative authority for the way of proceeding? A proximate answer to this question is provided by the timetable that the Government set out in October 2006, with the expectation that new unitary authorities would be 'up and running' by April 2009 (see Table 2.1). This timetable implies impatience on the part of the Government, an impatience with the possible delays and uncertainties involved in asking the Boundary Committee to examine specific areas and to make recommendations. If there were a national emergency, it would be possible to justify taking a short cut, but such a contingency would imply urgency in obtaining a very specific power. There was no emergency, and the retrospective powers were embedded in a Bill with wide and general significance, a Bill that took nearly a year in completing the parliamentary process. Consequently, the impatience shown by the government must be interpreted in a different way, as arising from the arrogance of power.

One might hope that the action taken ahead of legislation, with retrospective statutory endorsement, was a single event, not to be repeated, but that would be an error. One week before the 2007 Act with which we have been concerned came into force, another Act granting retrospective legality also became effective. Under the Sustainable Communities Act 2007, there are provisions for making procedural regulations and for issuing or revising guidance:

*Any consultation undertaken before the day on which this Act is passed is as effective as it would have been if undertaken after that date* (Section 5(7)).

The parallel with the 2007 Local Government Act is the following. In both cases, the Government was not consulting on whether to introduce legislation, and the form it might take; the consultation was about implementing future legislation, and therefore acting in the expectation that the Bill would pass. Retrospective authority was given for actions that, in the case of the LGR, the Government claimed it had the power to take under Common Law. Ordinary citizens would be entitled to think that the retrospective provisions show the Government to be aware that it has been taking liberties with the law, and with Parliament.

There is no room to doubt that the 2006-08 LGR and the associated legislative process provide a clear example of the way that the Government is prepared to take Parliament for granted, and that Parliament allows this to happen. If Parliament allows itself to be treated in this manner, then citizens are deprived of protection for their liberties. Furthermore, the way is open for the Government to be economical with the truth and to engage in active deception.

## Political deception

The Government was economical with the truth about the LGR, selective and inconsistent in its use of evidence, with the result that misleading impressions have been conveyed to local authorities, the public and Parliament. The pattern was so consistent that it could not have been accidental; if not accidental, then it must have been deliberate and therefore there was political deception (Oborne 2005, p. 7). This feature of the LGR was revealed by the DCLG itself with the November 2007 document, which purported to summarise the consultation responses on the LGR but did this in a thoroughly unsatisfactory way, clearly intended to convey impressions not supported by the evidence. Deception has been the hallmark of the LGR.

Unfortunately, this was not an isolated matter, an unwelcome exception to the general rule that the Government can be relied upon to provide accurate information and honest evaluations. With the fifth anniversary of the invasion of Iraq, a reputable journal that originally supported the military venture had this to say:

> *There may be a more general and insidious consequence of the war and the way Mr Blair justified it. The unwarranted confidence and dropped caveats, the cajoling of supposedly independent spooks: whether or not it qualifies as lying, the way the government, like America's, <u>manipulated the evidence</u> of Iraq's weapons of mass destruction, portraying a potential threat as an urgent one, was a scandal ... Yet the evidence of slipperiness and sloppiness that continues to drip out ... commands little attention. In part that is because the subject is tired and recondite. But the sad reality is that the mis-selling of the war confirmed rather than created a <u>widespread belief that ministers lie and spin rules</u>. The public's view of politicians was worryingly jaundiced even before Iraq.* (The Economist 22 March 2008, p. 42.)

The corroding impact of political deception was apparent during the LGR. The feeling was widespread that the Government could not be trusted, a matter serious enough in its own right. Given that the Government engaged in political deception, and given its failure to act as a tough but fair referee, those making proposals were tempted to make unreasonable claims, claims that in many cases they must have known were implausible. In some cases, when challenged, the response can only be described as hysterical, a determined defence of the original bid position because it was known that no serious challenge would be forthcoming from the DCLG. A considerable amount of misleading information was peddled, and some counties tried to prevent districts from commissioning polls and referenda. In the event, some local authorities got what they wanted not necessarily because their case was sound but because they played back to the DCLG the messages that the Government wanted to hear.

The deceptions employed by the Government elicited deceptions from many of the participants in the LGR process, thereby embedding the corruption yet further into the body politic. Whatever the final outcome of the process in terms of structural changes, it may well be the case that the most lasting effect of the LGR will prove to be the further debasement of probity in the way public affairs are conducted in England, a debasement the responsibility for which ultimately rests with the Government and with Parliament.

# Appendix

## LGR reports by Chisholm and Leach

### Chisholm and Leach
'Local government reorganisation in Cheshire: a critical appraisal'. Crewe & Nantwich and Congleton Borough Councils. June 2007.

### Leach and L. Pratchett
'Lincolnshire Pathfinder. Enhancing two tier working'. Lincolnshire CC and seven districts. January 2007.

### Chisholm
'Local Government Reform? A critique of the April 2006 INLOGOV document: *An Independent Review of the Case for Unitary Status. Oxford, Norwich, Exeter and Ipswich. Key regional cities'*. County Councils' Network, 27 October 2006.

'A unitary Authority for the whole of Somerset?' Five districts. 8 January 2007.

'One Council for Shropshire? A critique of the submission by Shropshire CC, Oswestry BC and S. Shropshire DC'. Shrewsbury & Atcham. 10 January 2007.

'A Critique of "One Somerset – One Council for Somerset"'. Five districts. 6 February 2007.

'A Critique of Wiltshire County Council's "We're Ready"'. Three districts. 6 February 2007.

'Affordability? A critique of "A Strong and Prosperous Exeter for All"' Devon CC. 27 March 2007.

'A Critique of the Financial Case Supporting "A New Council for North Yorkshire"'. Six districts. 18 April 2007.

"Critique of "One Cornwall One Council"". Four districts. 10 May 2007.

'An Examination of the Financial Case for a Unitary Co. Durham'. Seven districts. 11 June 2007.

# References

Chartered Institute of Public Finance and Accountancy (2006), *Finance and General Statistics 2006-07*. London: CIPFA.

Cheshire County Council (2007a), 'Local Government Reorganisation in Cheshire. A rebuttal of the work of Professors Leach and Chisholm, and of the Crewe and Nantwich Ipsos/Mori poll'.

Cheshire County Council (2007b), *Building a Sustainable Future*.

Cheshire Joint District Councils (2007a), 'Building a sustainable Cheshire. Cheshire County            Council's confirmation of its case for a single unitary authority in Cheshire'.

Cheshire Joint District Councils (2007b), *People and Places. The business case.*

Cheshire Joint District Councils (2007c), *East and West Cheshire 2-Unitary Bid. Response to Cheshire County Council Document for answer by 2nd November 2007.*

Chisholm M. (1975), *'The reformation of local government in England and Wales'*, in R. Peel,
M. Chisholm and P. Haggett (eds.), *Processes in Physical and Human Geography. Bristol essays*, 305-18. London: Heinemann.

Chisholm M. (2000a), 'Financial implications of major legislation'. *Public Money and Management*, 20:3, 21-26.

Chisholm M. (2000b), *Structural Reform of British Local Government. Rhetoric and reality*. Manchester: Manchester University Press

Chisholm M. (2002), 'The cost of local government structural reorganisation in Great Britain during the 1990s'. *Environment and Planning C: Government and Policy*, 20 251-62.

Chisholm M. and S. Leach (2007), 'Moving the goalposts for unitary structures'. *Municipal Journal*, 18 October, pp. 16-17.

Committee of Public Accounts (2007), *The Efficiency Programme: a second review of progress*, HC 349. London: Stationery Office.

Cornwall County Council (2007a), 'Response to Professor Chisholm's Critique of "One Cornwall One Council"'.

Cornwall County Council (2007b), *One Cornwall One Council*, Pt 1.

Deloitte (2007), *'People and Places'. Independent validation of the councils' submission supporting the financial case for reorganisation*. London: Deloitte.

Department for Communities and Local Government (2006a), *Strong and Prosperous Communities*. London: HMSO, Cm 6939-1.

Department for Communities and Local Government (2006b), *Invitation to Councils in England to Make Proposals for Future Unitary Structures; to pioneer, as pathfinders, two-tier models*. London: DCLG

Department for Communities and Local Government (2007a), *Proposals for Future Unitary Structures: stakeholder consultation. Summary of responses*. London: DCLG.

Department for Communities and Local Government (2007b), *Proposals for Future Unitary Structures: means of prioritising proposals*. London: DCLG.

Department for Communities and Local Government (2007c), *Proposals for Future Unitary Structures: stakeholder consultation*. London: DCLG.

Department of the Environment (1979), *Organic Change in Local Government*, Cmnd 7457. London: HMSO.

Jones G. and J. Stewart (2008), 'Why legislate when councils are already acting?' *Municipal Journal* 3 March, pp. 24-25.

Leach S., Davis H., Game C. and Skelcher C. (1991), *After Abolition: the operation of the post-1986 metropolitan government system in England*. Birmingham: Institute of Local Government Studies.

Lyons M. (2007), *Lyons Enquiry into Local Government*. London: Stationery Office.

Oborne P. (2005), *The Rise of Political Lying*. London: Free Press.

Price Waterhouse Coopers (2007), 'PWC Best Value Report', for Cheshire CC, June.

Royal Commission (1969), *Royal Commission on Local Government in England, 1966-1969*, 3 vols, Cmnd 4040. London: HMSO.

Select Committee on Economic Affairs (2008), *The Economic Impact of Immigration*, Vol. 1, *Report*, HL 82 - 1. London: Stationery Office.

Select Committee on Relations between Central and Local Government (1996), *"Rebuilding Trust"*, HL Paper 97 - I, Session 1995-96. London: HMSO.

Shropshire County Council (2006), *One Council for Shropshire*. Shrewsbury: Shropshire CC.

Wilks-Heeg S. and Clayton (2006), *Whose Town is it Anyway? The state of local democracy in two northern towns*. York: Joseph Rowntree Foundation.

# List of Tables

# Index

East Riding, 16

Electoral Reform Services, 92, 101

employment, 75

staff, 45-6, 65, 68, 75, 80, 99, 108

freedom of information, 83

Gershon savings, 5

Gershon, Peter, 5, 136

Great Yarmouth, 133

Greater London Authority, 142

Greater London Council, 139, 141, 144

Griffiths, Jan, 91, 93

gross annual savings, 56, 58-9, 62, 77, 79, 159

Gross Domestic Product, vi, 5

Hamill, Paul, 70

Healey, John, 17-18, 26, 51, 53-4, 62-3, 71, 83-5, 95, 114, 118, 119, 147

Hollis, Baroness, 128

Home Office, 6

House of Cammons

Committee of Public Accounts (2007), 5, 157

House of Commons, 5, 63, 83, 147

Select Committee on Economic Affairs (2008), 5, 158

House of Lords, 5, 24, 52, 83, 104, 106, 120, 128, 150

improved two-tier, 82, 93

information technology, 61, 64, 65, 79, 80, 85

Inner London Education Authority, 141

Ipswich, 9, 17, 19-21, 30, 32, 33-4, 39, 40-1, 54, 89, 115, 132, 154

Judicial review 89, 105-27

Kelly, Ruth, 137, 144

Lancashire, 16

Leach, Steve, iii, iv, vii, viii, 3, 4, 22, 57, 99, 141, 154, 156-7

Leeds, 131

legal challenge, 123